Perception and Deception

Perception
and
Deception

A Mind-Opening Journey
Across Cultures

Joe Lurie

Increase productivity • Strengthen relationships

Cultural Detective®
Nipporica Associates LLC
Leawood, KS 66206 USA

Visit our website at www.culturaldetective.com

ISBN: 978-0-9708463-6-5 (trade paperback)
ISBN: 978-0-9708463-5-8 (ebook)

DEDICATION

For Donna Rosenthal, my wife and journey-mate: your writer's wisdom, perspective, and support made *Perception and Deception* come to life.

And to our young nephews and nieces: Cy, Katie, Charlotte, Maya, Elias, Ari, Moriah, and Daniel, for whom the magic of the world's cultures awaits.

TABLE OF CONTENTS

FOREWORD

by Ambassador Martin Brennan, Retired

Shortly after we arrived in Kigali, Rwanda, in 1977, my wife and I hosted a lunch for her Rwandan hospital co-workers. As the dessert disappeared from the table, our guests glanced at one another and announced that they wanted to thank us for our hospitality. They stood up in unison and began clapping, singing, and dancing.

We'd never seen anything like this back home in California. After a moment, my surprise morphed into distinct cross-cultural concern. What was happening? And more importantly, what should we do? Were we expected to sit and smile? Sit and clap? Stand and clap? Or—heaven help us—join the dancing?

If only Joe Lurie's much-anticipated book had been available back then, I'd have recognized that this was an ideal moment to "go with the flow" and enjoy crossing cultures. *Perception and Deception* is a book of revelation and illumination, sparked by the wisdom the author gleaned while experiencing the world as a Peace Corps Volunteer, international program executive, intercultural teacher, trainer, and consultant.

Through poignant stories, comparisons of proverbs, insight into gestures, and gems of cultural-specific wisdom, Perception and Deception brilliantly illustrates the contrasts between cultures and our propensity to misinterpret unfamiliar cultural realities. To quote Joe's favorite African proverb: "The stranger sees only what he knows." We view the world through the blinders of our cultural assumptions.

Had I been able to don Joe Lurie's cultural lenses while serving in the diplomatic corps in Asia, Africa, and Europe, I would have seen and understood so much more about what was really being communicated, although unsaid. I might have received the deeper cultural messages that escape one who hears largely what one is used to hearing, and sees mostly what one is used to seeing. I would have better understood culture's influence on prejudice, stereotyping, status, and identity.

Joe Lurie conveys insights he's honed over decades of keen observation, research, and literally tens-of-thousands of conversations around the world. I've had the good fortune of being with Joe on some of these forays. One evening, when we were lost in Edmonton, Canada, Joe asked two strangers for directions. They turned out to be Japanese students and, within seconds, we were engulfed in a discussion of how people from different cultures give directions.

I once described to Joe how my hosts abroad often loaded food onto my plate despite my protestations that I was satiated. I relegated this phenomenon to the "strange quirks of foreigners"—a universal category, because at times, we are all foreigners. Eyes twinkling, Joe elucidated that in the U.S., a "clean" plate signals we've done our duty and wasted not; while, in much of the rest of the world, an empty plate signals that the guest is still hungry. Fulfilling my U.S. culturally instilled duty merely triggered guilt both in me, the guest ("How can I allow this food to go to waste?"), and in my host ("How can I leave this guest hungry?").

I didn't fully appreciate the pervasive influence of culture until I met Joe. Inspired by his work, I launched a course in cross-cultural communication at the University of California, Berkeley. When I was called to a diplomatic assignment, I asked Joe to take the reins. This ranks among my best decisions ever—akin to asking Fred Astaire to teach dancing. The course has become a popular mainstay under Joe's tutelage.

Speaking of Fred Astaire, my wife and I joined our dancing Rwandan guests as best we could. Our response proved to be culturally appropriate. Our initial trepidation in the next hour of dancing was transformed into friendship and community.

That afternoon I learned another Joe Lurie lesson: showing respect for another culture is infinitely more important than "doing it right." During his visit to Tokyo, President Obama may not have bowed in the inimitable style of the Japanese, but the fact that he made the effort when greeting the Emperor elicited accolades from the people of Japan. Those who wondered why President Obama would "bow" to anyone from another country could benefit from Perception and Deception, a mind-opening exploration of the pitfalls of seeing other cultures with "eyes wide shut."

For you, the reader, no matter your background or age, this exceptional book will expand your perceptions of other cultures—and your own—in fresh and exciting ways.

—Santa Margherita d'Adige, Italy

AUTHOR'S PREFACE
TO THE NEW EXPANDED EDITION

Think globalization is bringing us closer together? Think again.

With refugees crossing cultures lacking preparation, the dangers of intercultural miscommunication are intensifying. Why do many refugees traumatized by violence find Western "talk therapy" alienating? As a Syrian refugee confided, "I can't share my painful, humiliating stories with a stranger." A Sudanese refugee was diagnosed as "psychotic" because she seemed to be talking to herself; her Boston psychiatrist was unaware that in her world, conversing with ancestors is normal.

With YouTube, Tweets and fake news instantly crossing cultures without context, it's essential to understand the actual meanings and intentions behind words and actions that seem abnormal or provocative.

In our hyper-connected world, colliding cultures increasingly are causing misperceptions and misunderstandings. Some French see a Muslim woman in a *burkini*—a full-body swimsuit—as oppressed or a potential terrorist. Yet the woman considers her *burkini* liberating, because she can swim modestly.

Recently, a UC Berkeley student with a Spanish last name snidely was asked when she'd return to Mexico. Her angered response, "I'm from Kansas and don't speak Spanish."

Just as stereotypes fuel misunderstandings, different perceptions of "turbans' often result in intolerance and sometimes violence. Sikh men, who aren't Muslim or Hindu, often wear turbans, yet sometimes trigger thoughts of Bin Laden. Some American Sikhs have been killed because of this misperception. When an American Sikh UPS driver delivered packages, some customers called the police. He printed T-shirts with: "I'm a Sikh. Google it!"

In international business negotiations, is direct eye contact a sign of respect and engagement or disrespect, even aggression? Many Africans and Asians politely avert their eyes when speaking with elders or authority figures.

Why do Chinese and Japanese use many ways to avoid saying "no?" And when does "yes" really mean yes? That Thai client's smile: friendly, embarrassed or angry? And what are the possible interpretations of "soon" and "late" in Latin America? Those loud Israeli, Italian and Greek business colleagues: arguing and interrupting? Or simply talking?

And what do your experiences tell you when you're in line behind a bald man: A militant? A monk? A punk? A neo-Nazi...or a cancer patient?

In line, online and off-line, in this hyper-connected world we're meeting many more "strangers." There's new wisdom in the Lebanese proverb: "Every stranger is a blind man." And so, we face an urgency to teach students and professionals far more about other cultures and give them the intercultural skills to navigate globalization's turbulent waters.

Hoping to use the stories in this expanded new edition as springboards for developing intercultural competence,

I've added a broad array of interactive Questions and Activities at the end of each chapter, including this edition's new chapter, "Globalization and its Disconnects—Convergence Without Context." It focuses in large part on spiraling misunderstandings across cultures, especially in the worlds of religion, migration, and technology.

To better cope with the disrupting forces of globalization, each chapter includes "Questions and Activities" designed to develop and heighten cultural self-awareness and sensitivity to others among individuals, students, and groups of all backgrounds and professions. Some of the included interactive, personalized activities are available for those who choose to subscribe to *Cultural Detective*'s superb, research-based, internationally tested online platform providing access to nearly 70 packages of rich intercultural material.

For more information about this anytime, anywhere intercultural competence toolbox and virtual coach, visit www.CulturalDetective.com. To subscribe as an individual or group, go to www.CulturalDetective.com/cdonline.

EDITOR'S PREFACE

The team at *Cultural Detective* is extremely pleased to bring you *Perception and Deception*, an entertaining and enlightening read. Its goal matches that of our larger series: to build respect, understanding, and collaboration across cultures.

I met Joe Lurie several years ago in a facilitator certification workshop for *Cultural Detective* in Berkeley, California. Joe is a memorable guy: a consummate storyteller with a booming voice and a jovial sense of humor. His stories seemingly span every culture and just about every situation you can imagine. He talks with people about things I would never think of mentioning (for example, how often they wash their undergarments, or in what contexts talking about sex is okay). A conversation with Joe is hugely educational as well as full of belly laughs; he is a delight.

Imagine my pleasure when Joe asked me to work with him on this book, summarizing some of the major learning he's gained throughout a lifetime working across cultures! You are reading this book, no doubt, because you're interested in cross-cultural communication. Perhaps you straddle multiple worlds in your life, work with a team of people from distant locations, or love to travel. Whatever the reason for your interest, I know you will enjoy reading this volume as much as I have.

You'll find a wealth of stories and proverbs in this book, both items that are central to the *Cultural Detective* Method. *Cultural Detective* is a tool that helps people better understand their own cultural filters and those of others. It provides a process to work and live with people from different cultures in ways that bring out the best in each person, and harnesses the value that diversity can add to a team, organization, or community.

Cultural Detective is a collaborative project among over 150 authors worldwide. The series is used by multinational businesses, universities, NGOs, religious communities, professional associations, and individuals to improve their cross-cultural competence.

Please visit us at www.CulturalDetective.com.

AUTHOR'S PREFACE TO THE FIRST EDITION

When the first Europeans arrived in Africa and the Americas, some brought casks of red wine. Seeing these strangers drinking "blood" perhaps shocked some indigenous peoples, who may have considered them deranged barbarians. On the other hand, others like the Masai of East Africa, who frequently drink cows' blood, may have wondered what kind of cows these strangers "without color" owned.

Through my years working and traveling with "strangers" from over 100 countries, I've discovered that by relying on one's experiences and filters, a "perception" can actually be a "deception." To a mother who chews food before feeding the puree to her infant, an ad for Gerber baby food is bizarre. A Chinese elder who spits on the street is disgusted at seeing an Australian tourist blowing her nose in a tissue, then shoving the mucus-filled tissue into her purse.

Contrasting values across cultures, such as those mentioned above, are represented by the cow I chose for the cover of the first edition. The Masai, like many ethnic groups in Africa and in some other parts of the world, use cows for dowries because they represent wealth. Among Hindus, the cow is considered "divine," so sacred that it's often cared for in old age, and eating beef is forbidden. How strange this taboo appears to the many meat-eaters around the world who associate the cow with hamburgers, steak, or ribs—a divine dinner. But for many Hindus consuming a holy cow for dinner would be a disgrace.

I was inspired to write *Perception and Deception* because, for years, I've observed that "seeing" often can be "deceiving"—our experiences cause us to interpret a situation from our own point of view. When an Iraqi journalism student visited my office, he didn't sit with me at the table. I didn't realize that by standing, he was conveying respect. When I was the only "foreigner" on a boat with Tahitian fishermen, they often raised their eyebrows. Were they surprised, skeptical, or using "eyebrow language" to say yes? On a subway, I saw the back of a bald head and wondered: monk, punk, or patient?

After reading this book, when you perceive someone or a situation as peculiar, irrational, or offensive, I sincerely hope you'll pause before drawing quick conclusions. When we don't understand what is "normal" in another cultural context, our perceptions may be deceiving and may lead to misunderstanding that provokes laughter, tears, anger, or even violence.

With the increasing ease of international travel and mass migration, and with Tweets and YouTube videos going viral in seconds, the dangers of miscommunication across cultures are intensifying. In our interdependent world, more than ever, it's important to take time to understand the assumptions and intentions behind someone's words and actions.

Is the diplomat's hug an insult or a sign of warmth? When a man tells a prospective bride, "You're fat!" is that a slur? In some cultures, it's a compliment. Is the oncologist wearing a headscarf because she's a devout Muslim, or just having a "bad hair" day? During a business negotiation, is direct eye contact a sign of respect, disrespect, or aggression? Most anecdotes and observations in this book are drawn from my experiences with students, colleagues, immigrants, and friends from around the world. In some cases, I've changed names or modified circumstances to respect their privacy. But these are all true stories. I hope they are as revealing for you as they have been for me.

ACKNOWLEDGEMENTS

This expanded edition is in part inspired by the continued support in countless ways of Dianne Hofner Saphiere and *Cultural Detective*, my publisher. I am, as well, indebted to members of the Yazidi and other refugee communities, and to Shanti Corrigan, Charles Lam, David Lennon, and Muhammad Ali Shahidy for their invaluable contributions. Special thanks to Malcolm Evans for permission to publish his magnificent cartoon in Chapter Seven, to Katharine Ellis for her engaging cover design, and to the Author's Guild for its helpful guidance. As in the previous edition, I've changed or eliminated some names and modified circumstances in the interest of privacy.

May this edition's activities and reflections on the disrupting forces of globalization and migration offer positive paths for engaging with difference and ways of seeing with new eyes.

INTRODUCTION

Smelling Lions...But There Were None

My awareness about perceptions and misperceptions across cultures was born in the Entebbe, Uganda airport in 1967. I was en route to Kenya to serve as a Peace Corps Volunteer teacher.

Late at night, I left the plane and headed across the tarmac to the transit lounge. In the heavy, humid air, I smelled lions. I knew they surely were close...even though I never had smelled a lion. When I later learned that no lions were anywhere near the Entebbe airport, I began to realize that my senses had been tricked by many one-dimensional images of Africa.

This East African episode was the beginning of a life of intercultural encounters, filled with minefields and mind-openers. My experiences in Kenya—and other countries in Africa, Asia, Latin America, the Middle East, and Europe—often confused me. The limitations of my previous experiences had clouded my understanding of other cultural realities.

When, for example, my Tanzanian Swahili instructor casually held my hand during a fifteen-minute conversation, I felt very uneasy, confused by his intent. Was he gay? Later, I realized that this kind of physical contact among Tanzanian men has nothing to do with homosexuality, and, in fact, is quite common throughout Africa and in many countries around the world. I think I was just beginning to understand this fourth century Chinese poem:

How shall I talk of the sea to a frog if he has never left his pond?

How shall I talk of the frost to a bird of the summer land, if he has never left the land of his birth?

How shall I talk of life with a sage if he is the prisoner of his doctrine?

The stories I share in this book spring from my experiences and research across cultures, as well as from a long career in international educational exchange. They illustrate that, often, we don't see with our eyes, but, as this Chinese proverb suggests, "We see with what is behind our eyes"—through the prism of our limited experiences. Anais Nin put it this way: "We do not see things as they are; we see things as we are."

Consider footprints on a toilet seat. How many of us would be startled, perhaps disgusted, to see this? Yet, millions of people from different cultural upbringings understand why there are footprints, and wonder why anyone would even consider sitting on a toilet seat. Only when one leaves one's pond can both perceptions begin to make sense.

This book is about the confusion and clarity that can come with exposure to different cultures. It is meant to suggest the caution and wisdom of a Mongolian saying: "There are men who walk through the woods and see no trees."

The stories are accompanied by maxims and wise observations from around the world and across time. My hope is that they'll help put the cross-cultural encounters in perspective, and give them added life. As an Ethiopian saying puts it: "A proverb is to speech what salt is to food."

Ultimately, this journey of seeing beyond our shores, and understanding how others see us, will increase our understanding of ourselves, and the forces that shape who we are. This is illustrated so well by a Zen parable:

> Two tadpoles are swimming in a pond. Suddenly one turns into a frog and leaves the pond.
>
> When the frog returns to the water, the tadpole asks, "Where did you go?"
>
> "I went to a dry place," answers the frog. "What is 'dry?'" asks the tadpole.
>
> "Dry is where there is no water," says the frog. "And what is 'water?'" asks the tadpole.
>
> "You don't know what 'water' is?!" the frog asks in disbelief. "It's all around you! Can't you see it?"

CHAPTER ONE

African Awakenings

"The stranger sees only what he knows."
—Dogon West African proverb

Kerugoya, a small village with a few ramshackle shops near the base of Mt. Kenya, was my new home. The Peace Corps had found me a wooden, tin-roofed house, surrounded by avocado trees, near coffee and tea plantations. The house had no electricity or running water, but it did have a few small lizards in residence—quite a contrast from my cockroach-infested apartment in noisy New York City. I rarely saw cars during my fifteen-minute walk on a dusty road to the government high school for boys where I taught English, world history, and physical education to 15- and 16-year-old Kenyans.

Seeing my students strolling hand-in-hand confused me. As I was walking from the school to the village with a fellow teacher, six-foot-tall Githingu, he casually took my hand. I felt shocked and wanted to pull it away from him. But, remembering the lessons during my Peace Corps training, I didn't. While I understood that hand holding among men had nothing to do with homosexuality, it took months before I felt comfortable accepting or reaching out to take a man's hand during a stroll or extended conversation.

As my friendship grew with Githungu and two other male Kenyan teachers, Mwari and Kariuki, our conversations became more personal. But as weeks passed, I was surprised and hurt that my friends hadn't invited me to their homes. I'd never been inside a Kenyan home. I'd shown them photos of my family in New York. They knew homesickness made me crave my family's letters, my only link to home. (There was no Internet then, and only one phone in the village.) I wondered, did I offend my new friends? Or maybe they weren't willing to invite a Caucasian into their homes, given Kenya's British colonial history and Kenya's bloody armed struggle for freedom? Kenya had only gained independence from Britain in 1963, just four years before I arrived. Or perhaps they felt awkward about inviting a white man, generally perceived to be rich, into their modest homes?

As our friendship deepened, I invited my three colleagues to dinner at my house. They agreed without hesitation. As we ate, they appeared at ease. We discussed our eager students, who dreamed of entering the University of Nairobi. They peppered me with questions about the civil rights movement, and about the assassination of John F. Kennedy. We traded stories about teachers who'd inspired us. The entertaining evening ended on an up-note.

But the next few weeks were perplexing. They didn't offer a reciprocal invitation or even thank me. Again, I wondered if I'd said something that offended them. Or maybe a deeply rooted taboo prevented them from inviting a white man into their homes?

One night, the three of us were in a crowded bar where much of the village's social life took place. With the help of a few bottles of Kenyan Tusker beer, I mustered the courage to ask them if they'd enjoyed dinner at my home. When Mwari assured me they'd had a great time, I asked sheepishly, "Then why haven't you invited me to your homes?"

They looked surprised, explaining, "The door is always open!" So—invitations are not necessary! My mind was opening to the possibility of another reality. Days later, deciding to really see if "the door was always open," I knocked apprehensively on Mwari's door. His wife greeted me and, even though I told her I'd just eaten, her mother prepared *ugali*—cooked pounded maize and goat stew. I was more than welcomed.

During my three years in Kerugoya, whatever the hour, whenever I appeared at a friend's house, the door was always open. Each time I was greeted warmly and served a generous meal. So I learned that in Kerugoya, and in many other parts of Africa, my American notions of privacy, appointments, and schedules seemed strange.

Kenyans and I often misunderstood each other. When friends dropped by unexpectedly for a chat, I would ask what they'd like and rattle off choices of coffee or tea, fruit or cake, or whatever food I had. No matter what I offered, they either refused or didn't answer. Therefore, when my guests declined my offer of food, I didn't serve anything—unaware how inhospitable my behavior appeared, or how hungry they might have been. My customs blinded me to theirs.

It wasn't until my second year in Kerugoya that I realized why they didn't accept: even if they were hungry and thirsty, they didn't want to appear greedy. Guests never should be asked what they want, because it's the host's duty to feed them without offering any choices. When I started serving food and beverages without asking their preferences, my Kenyan guests always ate whatever I placed before them.

Recently, Solomon, an Ethiopian electrical engineer studying in California, visited our home. My wife, who'd met him in Ethiopia when he was twelve, asked if he was hungry. He said no.

She insisted he'd love the delicious pasta. Again, he insisted he wasn't hungry. Remembering my experiences in Kenya, I served him the pasta, which he ate readily. As a Ghanaian proverb puts it: "A stranger may have very big eyes, but he does not see what is going on with the people with whom he lives."

Last year, in San Francisco, I asked Okeke, a Nigerian friend, about some of his early misperceptions of life in the U.S. He described his confusion about hospitality when an American friend invited him to her "potluck" housewarming party. When Okeke arrived with three Nigerian friends and no food, the host appeared stunned. Okeke hadn't realized that in the U.S., housewarmings are usually for invited guests only, and "potluck" means "bring something to eat." He'd mistakenly followed a common Nigerian custom: it's insulting if a guest brings food, because it would imply the host isn't generous. At Nigerian housewarmings, friends and friends-of-friends usually are welcome. As Okeke explained, "uninvited friends bring warmth to the house."

In another food-related incident in Kenya, I was the only white man on a public bus traveling from a remote village to Nairobi. I was absorbed in a magazine when the elderly man sitting next to me poked my shoulder. He split his sandwich and offered half of it to me. What was the man's motive? I politely refused, unaware that if he didn't share his sandwich with me, he'd be considered selfish. How could this Kenyan know that to me, offering to share his food seemed strange and intrusive, but quite normal behavior for many Africans, especially in rural areas? Because of my upbringing in New York City, where many people value privacy and unsolicited offers from strangers are suspect, I didn't understand him. On this bus, I was the stranger, and could see only what I knew. As I started understanding the custom of sharing food with strangers on local buses, I became comfortable with accepting and sharing food with fellow passengers.

Shortly after returning to the U.S., I realized how much I'd changed due to living in Kenya. On a train trip from New York to Philadelphia, I was sitting next to a woman. Unwrapping a salami sandwich, I hesitated because I didn't know what to do. Then I chose the Kenyan way: I offered her part of my sandwich. Looking alarmed, she got up and changed seats.

While in Kenya and other countries in Africa, I frequently misinterpreted people's actions and words because I was seeing through my own individual "lens." When I visited outdoor markets, I'd often hear a Kenyan child call various women "mama," and refer to different men as "baba," (father, in Swahili). I knew the child was not related biologically to these people, and could only conjecture some bizarre anthropological kinship pattern. Later, when I lived in Ghana and traveled in Togo, Ivory Coast, Mali, Tanzania, and Uganda, I realized that in many African communities adults are seen as "collective parents" with shared responsibility for looking after children.

Another example of greatly differing perceptions occurred during a school vacation when I joined a team of U.S. American, Dutch, and British volunteers, along with ten Kenyan high school students, building a concrete elementary school near Lake Rudolf in northern Kenya. One night, during a group discussion around a campfire, a British volunteer bluntly criticized the Kenyan teens for their bad manners. A Dutch volunteer complained that the Kenyans were rude and didn't say "please" or "thank you."

A Kenyan student explained that because we were all part of one group, expressions like "please" and "thank you" were superfluous, even gratuitous. Because group cooperation and mutual support were expected, these expressions were unnecessary.

***

> *"If you go fast, you go alone.*
> *If you want to go far, go together."*
> —African proverb

In my intercultural classes at the University of California (UC), Berkeley, I tell my students the following African story. Their responses reveal differing perceptions about cooperation and competition.

> What do you think happened when children in an African community played this game?
>
> A basket filled with luscious fruit was placed near a tree in the distance. The children were told that whoever reached the basket first would win all the fruit.
>
> When the African children were told to run, they all joined hands and raced together. Then, they all sat together enjoying their treats.
>
> Asked why they had run as a group, even though one child could have won the entire basket of fruit, a boy answered: "How can one of us be happy if all the others are sad?"

Most of my European and U.S. students anticipated an exciting winner-take-all competition. When they learned the unexpected conclusion, their cultural expectations were jolted!

The story illustrates a South African saying, "I am because we are, and because we are, therefore I am." Quite a contrast to Descartes' "I think, therefore I am"!

The failure of individualists to perceive the power of group affiliation and identity can have serious, unintended consequences for aid and development workers. In parts of Africa, and other areas of the world, group identity takes precedence over individual, self-serving interests. A former U.S. diplomat told me that during a terrible drought in 2002, villagers in the south and west of Zambia were starving. Because the Zambian government was concerned about the safety of GMO maize, they cancelled a massive food aid program.

So, instead, USAID and the World Food Program sent emergency food aid directly and exclusively to families ravaged by HIV-AIDS. After about a month, evaluators were baffled because the afflicted people's nutrition levels hadn't improved as much as expected. A recipient explained, "It wouldn't be right for us to eat and not share with our neighbors. How can we eat separately from our community? We're all part of the same village."

In addition to the pervasive sense of community, I also was struck by the great respect African youth characteristically show elders. In youth-oriented societies, where people are bombarded by ads selling youth-promoting products, the implication is that aging is undesirable.

When I took my Kenyan students on their first trip to Nairobi, we met a 70-year-old U.S. American visiting professor at the University of Nairobi. One teen smiled and said, "Nice to meet you, Grandma." The professor was stunned by this unknown teen's temerity in referring to her as an old woman. Yet, for the Kenyan student, "Grandma" connoted great esteem for a wise elder who nurtures the young. As a Yoruba proverb from Nigeria puts it, "Respect the elders: they are our fathers."

Coming from the youth-obsessed U.S. culture, where expressions like "old woman" or "old man" usually are put-downs, I initially didn't understand that the Swahili word "*mzee*," which literally means "old man," is a term of reverence. A Kenyan saying, "The eye and ear can deceive its possessor," clearly described my own blinders and deafness.

Reverence for elders still is very important in Africa. Recently, I was driving a Nigerian history professor to the University of San Francisco, where we both were teaching. During the one-hour trip, his cell phone rang at least six times: people from his Ibo village in eastern Nigeria were requesting his advice on matters from marriage to money. Even though he lives in California most of the year, he retained his status as the most respected and sought-after elder in the village.

***

The Italian missionary headmaster at the high school where I taught often made negative comments about Africans. He derisively described our students as "apathetic," "dishonest," and "devious." When I asked him why he was so disdainful, he complained that when he spoke to the students, they said very little and never looked him in the eye.

Back in Rome, the headmaster was accustomed to verbal interaction with Italian students, so he didn't realize that the Kenyan students' silences conveyed respect. Clearly, he didn't understand the meaning of the African maxim, "A child among elders converses with his ears." People from cultures where eye contact is a sign of candor and confidence often don't recognize that African students' averted eyes commonly signify respect for an elder or authority figure.

Gradually, I learned that other nonverbal ways of communicating can also have dramatically different meanings around the world. For example, for years, I believed that a "thumbs up" was universally seen as a positive signal. It turns out, in Ghana, and many other countries of Africa and the Middle East, and also in parts of Italy, Greece, Brazil, and Australia, the "thumbs-up" sign is considered obscene. In Germany and Hungary, it can indicate the number one; in Japan, it can mean the number five.

It was surprising to learn that pointing with the index finger is considered rude in parts of Africa and Latin America, and in China, Japan, and Indonesia. Unknowingly, over the years, I have probably insulted and misunderstood people who had other correct ways of pointing. When, for example, friends from Central Africa, Madagascar, the Philippines, or Tahiti stuck out their lower lips to indicate a direction, I thought they were pouting because of something I'd said. Now, I understand that their lip gestures are just another way of pointing—and the polite way in their culture.

***

"More is meant than meets the ear."
—Chinese proverb

It was quite a discovery when I learned that the meaning of sounds varies across cultures. While living in Accra, Ghana, I heard loud hissing sounds, which I thought meant someone was being reprimanded. However, a Ghanaian businessman explained that this sound was a common way of calling a taxi. When I was traveling though Ethiopia, I often heard people making short, sharp, inward breaths, which I assumed were signs of asthma. Years later, I asked an Ethiopian medical doctor and friend why so many Ethiopians seemed to have asthma. She laughed and explained that these "gasping" sounds are a way of saying "yes" in her culture.

In most parts of Africa, drumming sounds often are associated with rhythm, dance rituals, or some kind of celebration. But in West African societies with tonal languages, the sounds of "talking drums" may simulate linguistic tone patterns, which can communicate a poem, a story, or the history of a people. You can hear these "talking drums" in parts of Nigeria, Senegal, Mali, Ghana, and Cameroon.

A former Peace Corps Volunteer in Nigeria told me that when he was traveling to a meeting in another village, his motorcycle broke down. He had to wait a long time, while people searched for parts to repair it. When he arrived late for the meeting, he was amazed that the villagers already knew the details of what had happened. Talking-drummers had conveyed the news about his motorcycle breakdown from one village to the next.

The first time I heard Miriam Makeba, the late, great South African singer, I heard clicking sounds, which I thought were some percussion instrument. I didn't realize that the various clicks are an integral part of the South African Xhosa language. On a YouTube video, Ms. Makeba demonstrates the "click song," and says many people ask how she makes "that noise." Her answer: "It's not a noise; it's my language."

Although I was becoming aware of my blindness about the varied meanings of gestures and sounds across cultures, it still took years to discover that I also was culturally color-blind. I didn't realize that specific colors might have a variety of meanings or connotations in different countries. For instance, in parts of South Africa and Ivory Coast, red suggests death; however, in parts of eastern Nigeria, red is associated with high rank and spirituality; and among the Kikuyu of Kenya, red connotes danger. Among the Fanti of Ghana, red may be associated with bloodshed, and yellow may suggest royalty. In Ghana, white can be associated with high rank, while in Ethiopia it may suggest mourning, and in Zambia, purity. The extraordinary variety and range of color-symbolism across Africa, and other parts of the world, often communicate messages that are incomprehensible to the outsider.

Even colors associated with genders can vary across cultures. Recently, a friend who is a U.S. American foreign-service officer in Burundi, joined a men's gym. He asked his driver where he could get a sturdy gym bag for his clothes. When the driver returned with a hot-pink bag, my friend, trying to hide his amazement and disappointment, smiled politely. He wondered whether the color was meant to convey a hidden message, and worried how he'd be received at a men's gym with the hot-pink bag. The next day, at a meeting with businessmen and high-ranking government officials, he was relieved to see several men wearing pink shirts. While pink and blue don't have gender associations in Burundi today, the story reminded me of Burundi's former colonial connection to Belgium, where pink is still often associated with boys, and blue with girls.

***

"Too much speed breeds delay."
—Shona proverb (Zimbabwe)

I was discovering the languages of color, sound, and gesture, I also learned there are different languages of time—not all cultures are governed by the clock, or by schedules and deadlines. Often, while in Africa, I heard someone say, "I can do that just now." Eventually, I learned that "now" could mean tomorrow, or next week, or some vague time in the future.

During a semester abroad program for U.S. university students in Ghana, we joined a week-long construction project in the countryside, helping to build a new infirmary. One evening after work, the village chief invited us to attend a play based on a traditional folk tale. The chief told us to arrive at "about" nine p.m. We arrived promptly at nine. We chatted with local villagers around a campfire until 9:45 p.m., when singers and musicians arrived and started serenading us as a preamble to the play. We enjoyed the music, but at about 10:15 p.m., we wondered when the play would begin. By 10:30 p.m., we became uneasy and increasingly frustrated. At about 11 p.m., I asked the chief when the play would begin. He responded, "Just now; only ten more songs and we'll get started!"

This true story reminds me of an Ethiopian proverb, which makes a similar point: *"If one is not in a hurry, even an egg will start walking."*

Speaking of walking, my walks in the Tanzanian countryside gave me insights into different concepts of time and distance. When I took a bus from the capital, Dar es Salaam, to visit an outdoor museum displaying traditional architectural styles of homes, I asked the driver to drop me off near the museum. After about an hour, he signaled me to get off, and pointed ahead saying, "It's just down the road." The bus veered off in a different direction, and I started walking down the dirt road. After ten minutes, I asked a farmer carrying bananas if I was almost there. He responded, "It's just down the road." During the next 45 minutes, I asked four more people, and each gave me the same answer: "It's just down the road."

After walking almost an hour, I decided I was the victim of some colossal joke. Just then, I finally spotted the museum. When I asked the museum's manager why people told me, "it's just down the road," he chuckled and explained: for people used to walking two-to-three hours a day to work or school, "just down the road" means it's close.

Years later, I related this story to a friend, originally from a northern Nigerian village, and he recalled his own misperceptions of "distance." When he arrived in New York City, he asked a woman for directions to the nearest public library. She responded, "It's not far, just a few blocks. Only a few minutes away." My Nigerian friend walked five blocks beyond the library, still thinking it was at least many more blocks further.

Feeling lost or confused in a new environment is a common experience for all of us. The Swahili word for Europeans is *"wazungu,"* which originally meant "people who waste time going around and around in circles." This word reflects how East Africans must have perceived the first Europeans who arrived in the region: lost people with no sense of direction.

***

"The truth is helpless when up against perception."
—Zack W. Van

My struggles in Africa, trying to understand perceptions of time and distance, remind me that many U.S. Americans hold distorted ideas about Africa. The U.S. news media rarely covers Africa. There are only a few U.S. American journalists based in Africa, and most cover only fighting, famines, or diseases.

Many U.S. students think Africa is a country, not a continent, and that Africa is about the same size, or slightly larger, than the U.S. Most of my students are astonished to learn that Africa is about three-and-a-half-times larger than the continental U.S. In fact, Africa is larger than the United States, China, India, Japan, and all of Europe—combined. Many U.S. maps give an ethnocentric, distorted picture of the size of the U.S. in comparison with other countries of the world.

A nation's films, like its maps, can produce distorted impressions. To this day, Tarzan movies have left distorted images of Africa as dominated by jungles, although less than fifteen percent of Africa is jungle or rainforest. A Zimbabwean visiting scholar at UC Berkeley told me that an American student asked how he gets up his tree at night. The exasperated Zimbabwean answered, "I take the elevator!"

Not much has changed since the Tarzan movie days. Gitau, a university-educated mechanical engineer from Nairobi, his wife, and 17-year old daughter are astonished by questions Americans ask them such as, "Do you live with zebras?" "Where do you go hunting?" "Do you live in the jungle?" "How did you escape being eaten by lions?" "Do you wear clothes at home?" They're from Nairobi, a city of about six million people, with skyscrapers, shopping malls, and an ice skating rink.

As old Tarzan films have distorted our concept of Africa, I was surprised at the popularity of cowboy movies in my Kenyan village. This was probably what prompted one of my Kenyan students to ask me, who was born and raised in New York City, "Who is taking care of your horse?"

Gitau told me that American cowboy movies are frequently shown throughout Kenya. In 2014, six months after immigrating to the U.S., he still wondered why he hasn't seen any horses or cowboys. Gitau also confirmed there is a popular Kenyan stereotype about Americans: they are so fabulously rich they don't need to work. He was amazed to see many Americans working long hours, observing that those who did not work were on welfare, without health insurance, or even homeless.

Perhaps even more startling is the story that Maurice, an architect/real estate developer and International House (I-House) alumnus from Ghana, told one of my UC Berkeley classes:

One summer, during my sophomore year, I saw a work-study job ad for a lab assistant position at the Lawrence Berkeley lab in the hills above the UC campus. I phoned and left a message expressing my interest in the job. When I got home, one of the lab staff had left a message on my answering machine, asking if I could come immediately to the lab since they thought I would be a good fit for the job.

Excited about the opportunity, I went up there and met the hiring person. She was visibly excited when she saw me. She told me the job involved taking care of various lab animals, including tarantulas, snakes, and at least one boa constrictor. She told me that occasionally the boa constrictor escaped and all I needed to do was to grab it and put it back inside its cage. Looking up at me with a smile, she told me the staff was excited when they got my call, and could tell from my accent that I was African. They figured handling animals must be something normal for me, and that they'd like me to start right away.

I was too horrified of the animals to even try to correct their erroneous assumption. Instead, I tried my best to keep my composure and responded in the affirmative, while looking for the opportunity to disappear from the lab. On the contrary, I'd never even seen a tarantula before. And the only times I'd seen snakes were when my elementary school class visited the zoo back in Ghana.

After I left, they kept calling me four or five times, over several days, to come start the job. I was too horrified to call them to tell them I was not interested.

As Alan Alda aptly observed, *"Your assumptions are your windows on the world. Scrub them off every once in a while, or the light won't come in."*

Questions and Activities, Chapter One

1. Consider the African proverb that begins the chapter: "The stranger sees only what he knows." Think about a time when you saw something and thought it was something else; when you misinterpreted a person, experience, or thing because you viewed it through one lens and not another. Then, reflect on when someone may have perceived you through the lens of what they knew, misunderstanding your experience or intentions. If you have a subscription, log into your account on *Cultural Detective Online*, enter into a corresponding package and click on "Create your own Incident" to record your story and debrief it in order to make meaning from it.

2. Watch the TED talk on YouTube, "The Danger of a Single Story," by the Nigerian writer Chinamanda Ngozie Adichie, at http//www.ted.com/talks/ chimamanda_adichie_the_danger_of_a_single_story .

    What does her presentation suggest about the origin and nature of stereotypes? How might her comments apply to notions and assumptions about Africa and Africans, as well as to any group of people? If you have a subscription, log into your account on *Cultural Detective Online*, and click on "Add Note" to journal your thoughts.

3. Interview a student or immigrant from an African country. What are some of the mistaken notions about Africa and Africans that your interviewee has encountered when interacting with people who have never set foot on the African continent? This is another good chance to log into your account on *Cultural Detective Online*, enter into a corresponding package and click on "Create your own Incident." Have your interviewee help you write the story and analyze it. You both might learn something transformative!

4. What kind of associations do you have with the words "old" and "old person?" Can you think of a time when you thought of "old" positively? Negatively? Where do these associations come from—what in your experience taught you to view "old" the way you do? Log into your account on *Cultural Detective Online*, click on the *Self Discovery* package, and record the values and beliefs you hold around youth, old age and aging. Next, reflect on what differing reactions to the word "old" tell us about the values of the people who hold them. Discuss these with your family, friends and colleagues.

5. Describe a gesture or sound you have used which may have annoyed or even provoked another person. Log into your account on *Cultural Detective Online*, enter into a corresponding package and click on "Create your own Incident" to record your story. What were the meanings you intended to convey and what were the messages that you unintentionally may have conveyed? Add that information into the Worksheet for your Incident in *CD Online*, along with strategies for how you could have bridged the differences in that situation.

6. Watch the YouTube video by Philip Zimbardo, "The Secret Powers of Time," https://www.youtube.com/watch?v=A3oIiH7BLmg. How in your experience have different conceptions of time contributed to misperceptions and misunderstandings across cultures? Reflect on a time in your life when different understandings of the meaning of time affected you: you arrived "late," or you were "in the moment" while someone else was planning for the future. Log into your account on *Cultural Detective Online*, and either record and debrief your story so you learn more about yourself, others, and how to bridge time differences, or enter the *CD Self Discovery* package and enter some of your values and beliefs around time for use in your Personal Values Lens.

CHAPTER TWO

Close Encounters of a Cross-Cultural Kind at the University of California, Berkeley's International House

"The International House concept is the first large-scale attempt to integrate the human race since the Tower of Babel."
—Harry Edmonds, co-founder of the
International House movement

Harry Edmonds inspired the first major International House, in New York City, in 1924, with financial support from John D. Rockefeller, Jr. He came to Berkeley a few years later, looking for a site to build a second International House, and found Piedmont Avenue, lined with fraternities and sororities, which at that time excluded foreigners and people of color. Seeking to strike bigotry "right hard in the nose," Edmonds chose Piedmont Avenue.

Today, Berkeley is known as a liberal city, so it's hard to believe that back in 1928, I-House was a radical idea: international and American students—men and women of all colors—living together under one roof. Property owners feared I-House would cause Berkeley to be "overrun" with blacks and Asians. Remember, in those days, black students couldn't even get their hair cut on campus.

The Berkeley Improvement Association was adamantly opposed to the construction of International House, according to a 1928 article in *The Courier*, a Berkeley newspaper. Its members feared that this revolutionary, interracial, and co-educational living center would attract "leprous spots," (dark-skinned people) as well as "swarming Asiatics." In addition to hostility towards foreigners and "colored" people living in an integrated building with "whites," many Berkeley landlords feared a drop in property values.

The anger against the proposed racially integrated International House was so intense, that in 1929, more than eight hundred people gathered in downtown Berkeley to protest its opening. Delilah Beasley, a black reporter for the Oakland Tribune, passionately defended the concept to the stunned audience. She said that American white prejudice was caused by a lack of contact with other groups of people.

International House at the University of California, Berkeley, opened in 1930. It is one of the largest, most diverse residential cultural program centers in the U.S., second only to the International House in New York City. Strategically, about thirty-five percent of I-House residents are U.S. citizens and permanent residents. This offers Americans an opportunity to learn about the rest of the world and gives international students a welcome to American life.

I-House faces toward the Pacific Ocean, a symbolic joining of East and West. The first director of I-House, Allen Blaisdell, hoped the new residence would draw Asian students—particularly Chinese, Japanese, Filipinos, and Indians—from their semi-ghetto housing in Berkeley, into an international community. And it did.

I-House was so unusual that in 1931, tour buses from San Francisco stopped in front so gaping passengers could stare at all the "strange" people. Some I-House residents were so resentful that when tour buses arrived, they hopped around pretending to eat grass, as if they were zoo animals. Indeed, for the next three decades, I-House often was called "the zoo."

***

"The world is a beautiful garden where truth,
like flowers, unfolds in different ways."
—Harry Edmonds, co-founder of the International House movement

I enjoyed twenty eye-opening years as Executive Director of International House, located in an imposing Spanish Moorish-style building at the top of the University of California, Berkeley campus. "I-House," as it's commonly called, was founded on the idea that friendship can transcend nationality, race, and religion. As a blonde Californian, who speaks fluent Mandarin and French, put it: "Everyone moves in here with prejudices. But here we slam ourselves head-on into them—at the dinner tables, in the elevators, in the library." In this living cross-cultural laboratory, about 65 percent of the residents are international; the rest are from the U.S. Many students from the U.S. have lived or traveled abroad; others have never befriended a foreigner or owned a passport.

In this cultural and residential center, scenes of "smashing stereotypes" are not unusual. For some residents, I-House is the first place they've lived outside their countries. A Japanese student asked an African-American student from Detroit why African Americans like fried chicken and watermelon so much. His response: "I'm a vegetarian. And as for watermelon, well, having friends from all over the world is teaching me that it's not only in the U.S. that

African-Americans are victims of unfair media representation."

Many students and scholars become aware of their national, ethnic, religious, or socio-economic blinders during their stay at I-House. Francisco, who once swept floors in a shoe factory in Guanajuato, says moving into I-House was a social shock.

"In Mexico, people of my class don't mingle with the rich. It took me a while to feel comfortable eating with students who talk about skiing in Switzerland and beach houses. I'm trying to teach them about Mexico—that it's not all like Tijuana." Raising money for scholarships is the nonprofit institution's way of helping residents cross class, as well as national borders. Part of the I-House experience is having students who grew up in families that can only afford rice and beans socialize with students who grew up with private chefs. Where else can the son of a Cuban refugee go salsa dancing with his roommate, the Crown Prince of Norway?

***

"A fence between makes love keener."
—German proverb

When I-House was founded, people in Berkeley feared that having men and women living together under one roof would promote "mixed marriages." And in fact, many of the first interracial and cross-national marriages in the San Francisco area were "born" at I-House. In fact, over the years, there have been hundreds of cross-cultural I-House marriages. The former Canadian ambassador to Iran, who helped the American hostages escape, and his Chinese-

Australian wife met at I-House. A Moroccan UN official at the Security Council met his Dutch wife at an I-House party. Some cross-cultural romances are not easy. When an Indian Hindu woman and a Pakistani Muslim man became serious, both sets of parents were miserable. "My father always said no Muslim would ever enter our house," she recalled. "And his mother looked down on dark-skinned Indians like me." She described their love affair as "Romeo and Juliet gone nuclear."

***

A Chinese-Brazilian student asked a Czech female friend to find him a room in I-House with "anybody except an Indian." (In the 1960s, Indians were stereotyped, not as software developers and medical doctors, but as snake charmers, cow worshippers, and cab drivers). The semester was starting and the only room available was with an Indian graduate student. Reluctantly he moved in and discovered his Indian roommate "wasn't so bad." The three became close friends and two years later, the Czech woman and the Indian married.

Different values can clash in challenging but revealing ways in intercultural romances. Two graduate students, a Haitian and an American, were deeply in love. She enjoyed Haitian music and dance and was fascinated by his deep spiritual belief in voodoo and the devotional objects he kept in his room. When they went for a romantic walk on the beach one day, he told her he'd gone to the butcher shop and bought an offering for the goddess of the ocean, the mother of all life. She wasn't surprised. She was aware that he respected mysterious spirits, each one responsible for a particular aspect of life. He unwrapped a package and proudly showed her his offering of respect for the goddess. "Filet mignon? You don't have much money," she protested angrily. "Why couldn't you offer hamburger?" Ignoring her, he walked towards the waves and tossed the filet mignon offering into the Pacific Ocean. Here was a case of spiritual and material values at odds with each other.

A Chinese student was surprised that men often visited her American roommate. "After midnight, I was in the bathroom. When I got to our room, I heard a man's voice. I returned to the bathroom and stayed there for an extra forty minutes. My roommate didn't realize how awkward I'd feel meeting a man in my nightgown. American students are so much more casual about these matters."

***

"When you look at me, do you see me?"
—from the movie *Focus*, based on Arthur Miller's 1945 novel about racism and anti-Semitism

Living in such an extraordinarily diverse environment, students often are amazed to discover how stereotypes affect both how others see them, and how they see themselves. Senar, a Turkish PhD student, told me that I-House residents usually don't believe he's Turkish, because he has blonde hair and green eyes. A third-generation Indian-American is often asked what part of India she's from. When she answers, "Boston," the common response is: "But where are you REALLY from?" Many other students express similar frustrations.

"Here I meet people from countries I've only read about in National Geographic, from Bhutan to Bolivia," says Tokeshi, an effusive third-generation Japanese-Brazilian. He had his first cross-cultural adventure in the dining room. "I sat with a guy with an Asian face like mine but was shocked when he said he's from Los Angeles. I just assumed all Asians were foreign students like me." Students are astonished when they find out Tokeshi is from São Paulo, until he explains that Brazil has the world's largest community of overseas Japanese. Tokeshi said that making Japanese friends for the first time gives him insight into his grandparents' heritage, yet also helped him realize how Brazilian he is. "When I started hugging a Japanese friend, she recoiled. That's when I realized hugging is an offensive greeting in Japan."

After a Tanzanian engineering student performed an energetic, spirited African harvest dance at an I-House talent show, her friends from the Philippines, Norway, and the U.S. asked for a lesson. After showing them just a few basic movements, she was stunned: the residents danced with exuberance and unexpected rhythmic skill.

A British student, Nadine, frequently was asked what part of Africa she came from. Students often were taken aback when she replied, "North London." And in the Queen's English, she would explain she'd never visited Africa.

Some French students told me how disarming it is to meet a student from Texas who plays Beethoven sonatas beautifully on the piano and discusses Jean Paul Sartre with ease.

An American journalism student asked a staff member from Madagascar what exotic custom the grey smudge mark on her forehead represented. The answer? It was from Ash Wednesday, a Christian tradition.

Despite many years living abroad, working as an intercultural trainer, and serving as Executive Director of I-House, I realize how stereotypes unconsciously affect my own assessment of people from other cultures. A Sicilian student made an appointment to see me, to discuss a problem with her roommate. Having vacationed in Sicily, I assumed she'd arrive late, so I made a phone call. When she came to my office promptly at 11 a.m., I was surprised. "I know," she said. "I'm a blue-eyed, blonde Sicilian, and I'm on time."

***

"Time waits for no man."
—German proverb

"Give time to time."
—Italian proverb

I-House students can have dramatically different perspectives about time. Heinz, a German visiting scholar in physics, described his first date with Maria, a sociology student from El Salvador. They were to meet at her I-House room at 8 p.m. Maria, aware of the German reputation for strict punctuality, was expecting Heinz to arrive at about 7:45; Heinz, aware that much of Latin America has a more elastic approach to time, didn't arrive until 8:45. They laughed with me as they described their good intentions.

Their miscommunication was because both were aware of the other's cultural approach to time. Perhaps that's why today they're happily married.

Still, for many Greeks, Spaniards, and others who live in the Olive Oil Belt, where it's customary to eat dinner as late as 10 or 11 p.m., adjusting to the appallingly early U.S. American dining hours of 5:30 to 7 p.m. is difficult. After discussions with the I-House student council, we decided to extend dinner hours to 8 p.m. But our American dining room staff protested that they needed to be home with their families, while the Spanish students, who enjoyed lengthy dinner conversations, complained that closing the dining room at 8 p.m. was outrageously early.

Different perceptions about party times also cause conflict. Weekend parties at I-House end by 2 a.m., to keep the noise levels down for other students. I'll never forget when a brilliant Brazilian visiting math professor angrily accused me of being "a fascist." For him—and students from a number of countries—parties begin at 11 p.m., and should end, naturally, in the early morning. Just as the Brazilian scholar came to understand different approaches to time, so U.S. residents traveling in Brazil learn to look at clocks in a new way.

***

"The tree remembers long after the ax forgets."
—Chinese proverb

Face-to-face encounters at International House don't always overcome the dangers of stereotyping. A Turkish student told me that after an off-campus party ended, she offered an Italian law student a ride back to I-House. The Italian woman refused, saying, "My Armenian grandparents would roll over in their graves if they knew I even said hello to you." The Turkish student was shocked. Aside from the unjust assumption that all Turks of all generations are responsible for the Armenian genocide (which some Turks still deny), their encounter had a painful irony: the Turkish student's mother is a Serbo-Croatian Jew, and her father is a Greek Christian from Cyprus.

Misperceptions based on students' appearances, religion, or nationality reached dramatic heights during the days after 9/11. While walking on the UC campus, Raj, an economics student with dark skin, dark hair, and thick eyebrows, recalls some hostile looks and gestures. He was stung by a student's ugly comment: that he looks like an Arab terrorist. Raj was born in the U.S. His mother is Mormon; his father is a Hindu.

A former I-House staff member, a Muslim originally from Iran, told me that a few weeks after 9/11, an FBI agent arrived at her front door. He demanded: "Where's the anthrax?" Apparently, a plumber who'd made repairs in her kitchen had alerted the FBI that he'd spotted a suspicious white powder. The FBI found the powder. It was sugar. There was an Arabic-speaking man in the house: her husband, an Iraqi Jew.

Stereotypes can negatively influence perceptions and poison relations across cultures. To fit into life in the U.S., and her undergrad dorm at UC Berkeley, Dina converted from Islam to Christianity, and attended church with several of her American dorm friends. But after the attacks of 9/11, these friends turned on her. "I thought all Americans hated me because I'm Middle Eastern, so I hated all Americans back with passion," she recalled. "If they gave me dirty looks, I returned them."

To avoid American students, Dina moved into I-House, which she mistakenly thought was exclusively for non-Americans. When she discovered her roommate was Caucasian from Alabama, she was shattered and afraid, because she believed all white Southerners were conservative and racist.

After a few cautious days of living together, Dina gradually realized her roommate, an art student, was warm, thoughtful, and open-minded. Eventually, they became close friends. "My experiences with her and life at I-House changed me," said Dina. "Now when I feel prejudice, I don't hate back. I know it's one person's ignorance, not the ignorance of an entire nationality."

***

> *"There is no reality except the one*
> *that is contained within us."*
> —Herman Hesse

Sometimes face-to-face encounters reveal surprising gaps of knowledge. Paolo, an Italian mathematician, had lived a sheltered village life. He'd never left Northern Italy, never met a non-Italian, or even a non-Catholic. After earning the highest math scores in Italy, he won a scholarship to UC Berkeley. Paolo described entering his I-House room in the 1950s. His roommate was asleep. The next morning Paulo recalled waking and was stunned to see a "tall, olive-skinned stranger with a long beard. He was combing his dark hair, which came down to his waist. I was trembling. I thought, 'he's Jesus Christ!'" Paolo's roommate rolled his hair on top of his head and covered it with a turban. His Sikh religion, he explained, forbids men from cutting their hair, as it is a gift from God. That encounter was the first time Paulo had ever heard of the Sikh religion.

Different perceptions and values also can cause thought-provoking ethical debates. During dinner, a Kuwaiti student's friends gave him a birthday surprise: a scantily clad Egyptian belly dancer wearing beads and sequins stepped onto a dining room table, and started gyrating to loud rhythmic, repetitive music. Hundreds of delighted students clapped to the rhythms, enjoying the hip action of this spirited cultural dance. "Diversity in action," a student called it. But the next morning, I received a petition signed by several American and European feminists. They were outraged by the belly dancer; they said it encouraged the "objectification and exploitation of women." In the spirit of I-House, instead of a blowup over the exotic entertainment, the incident set off a spirited dialogue in which each side was able to consider other points of view.

Several years later, International House hosted a dinner celebrating the Persian New Year, *Norooz*, a three-thousand-year-old spring festival of renewal and rebirth. Students ate traditional dishes such as *pulav*, rice enriched with nuts and saffron, *and chahar shanbeh soori*, a special soup of roasted garbanzo beans, almonds, pistachios, hazelnuts, dried figs, apricots, and raisins.

Again, when a scantily clad woman performed an undulating Persian dance, residents clapped enthusiastically. But in the corner, I noticed about twenty uneasy Chinese students warily watching, intrigued at this strange dancer showing so much flesh in public. I braced myself for another student protest. Rather, suddenly a Chinese student ran forward and began gyrating sinuously with the dancer, both moving their upper bodies with abandon. As hundreds of residents cheered, the hesitant Chinese students, as if granted permission, shot photos and videos, non-stop.

***

"The real voyage of discovery consists not in seeing new lands, but in seeing with new eyes."
—Marcel Proust

When Sophie, born and raised in San Francisco, came to my office, she was upset and confused. She urgently needed my advice because she knew I'd spent years in Africa. She was working on a sociology project with a fellow resident from Ghana. The night before their joint class presentation, Sophie went to Amma's room so they could practice together. When they finished, Sophie said, "See you tomorrow morning," and headed down the hall.

Wearing only her pajamas, Amma walked Sophie to the third-floor stairwell. Instead of saying goodbye there, Amma followed Sophie up the stairs to the fourth and fifth floors. Sophie became increasingly anxious as Amma tailed closely behind her to the sixth and seventh floors. When they reached the eighth floor, Sophie was nervous, fearing Amma was communicating a sexual interest. Sophie hurried to her room, but Amma shadowed her. When Sophie reached her door, Amma said, "See you in class." Panicky, Sophie entered quickly and abruptly closed the door on Amma, to prevent any unpleasantness.

Sophie apologized to me for the urgent meeting but said in two hours she'd be making her class presentation with Amma. She hoped I could explain: Was Amma's "bizarre" behavior sexual? Or "some strange African thing"? Because

I'd lived in Ghana for four months, I knew that it's common for hosts to accompany their departing guest, not just to the door or gate, or even to their car, but to walk them home, even if it was to another village. When I told Sophie that Ghanaians are among the most hospitable, welcoming people I'd ever met, she seemed enormously relieved, her eyes opening to a new reality.

To check the accuracy of my explanation, I met with Amma and told her how fondly I remembered my friends in Ghana walking me all the way home late at night. That's how we treat guests, she said, confirming that the explanation I'd given Sophie was accurate. When I asked Amma if some Americans were ever confused by Ghanaian-style customs, she said yes, especially when she used her hands to pick up mashed potatoes to sop up stew. Being asked questions about their country's cultural traditions forces a number of students to examine aspects of their own cultures they take for granted. "A big part of living here," Amma told me, "is discovering who you are."

***

"Discovery consists of looking at the same thing as everyone else and thinking something different."
—Albert Szent-Gyorgyi, Nobel Prize winner in physics

Numerous International House residents come from countries where homosexuality is commonly seen as blasphemy and is condemned, and, therefore, is a topic to avoid. Many students in the late 1990s were shocked when the annual Valentine's Dance posters, with images of male and female couples dancing, were torn down or vandalized. Someone scrawled, "WE EXIST, TOO!" across one poster.

On another poster, someone added symbols for gay and lesbian couples.

In response, a new poster was put up with references meant to reflect the I-House mission of inclusiveness: symbols for heterosexual, gay, lesbian, and transgender couples.

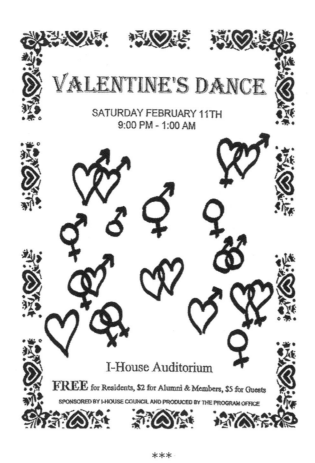

***

"He who sees one side only, sees nothing."
—Anonymous

In 1924, the founding logo of the International House movement was a ship sailing between the continents. In the 1990s, a group of African-American residents asked me what the logo meant. I explained that the ship was designed to convey an image of students travelling between countries to spread the spirit of the International House motto: "That brotherhood might prevail."

To these African-American students, the sailing ship triggered an ugly association: slave ships. Many residents had never looked at the logo through this prism; some pointed out that many sailing ships weren't involved in the slave trade. Still, the image was such a painful reminder for some residents of African descent, that I-House Berkeley removed the sailing ship from the logo.

Many international residents have had limited or no contact with African-Americans until they live in I-House. When Jeffrey, an African-American from Detroit, opened the door to his room, his new roommate from Hong Kong looked shaken and upset at having a black roommate.

"Despair filled my soul, Jeffrey recalled. At first I thought, 'I want out.'

For the first few days we barely talked. Then, after I unpacked several Chinese language books, he asked why. When I answered in Mandarin, he was shocked. We talked until dawn. It led to many cross-cultural talks between us, covering Chinese customs, travel, romance, and African-American culture. Our cross-cultural chats made us aware of our commonalities and differences.

Right before Christmas vacation, he asked, with all the sincerity of a father's fear of losing a son, if I'd continue being his roommate next semester. Of course I said yes. Friendship is an evolutionary process."

International Dining Differences

"It's darkest under the lighthouse."
—Japanese proverb

The large International House dining room is divided into two sections: one window-lined and brightly lit; the other has dark walls and soft lighting. Residents often asked me why I thought Asian students tend to eat in the brightly lit, window-lined section of the dining room, while students from other parts of the world generally congregate in the section with subdued lighting. Though it was not surprising that residents often like to socialize with others from the same culture and who speak the same language, I couldn't explain why, year after year, most Asian students consistently ate in the brighter section.

Then a graduate student told me he'd discussed the "mysterious" dining behavior with his parents. His Chinese father explained that many Asians consider the way food looks as important as its taste; they prefer bright light so they can see the food better and enjoy the complete dining experience. His Caucasian-American mother explained that she associated soft lighting with dinner. She preferred eating in dimly lit Western restaurants; her husband favored brightly lit Chinese restaurants.

Did I-House students instinctively gravitate to a section of the dining room that most closely resembled the lighting they were accustomed to? When I offered this explanation to residents in succeeding years, they readily agreed, saying it "makes sense."

It was as if unconscious patterns of behavior across cultures, once little understood, had been exposed to the light of discovery.

***

"One man's meat is another man's poison."
—Lucretius

In the dining room at I-House, a Ukrainian graduate student discusses Putin with a mathematician who has a thick Arkansas accent. At another table, a white Afrikaner and a black South African share stories of being homesick. Close to 600 students and scholars from over 80 countries—Mongolia to Jamaica to Argentina—call I-House home. An Iraqi, an Israeli, and an Iranian may sit together for the first time at a dinner table halfway across the world, discussing their fears, and their favorite Bart Simpson jokes. When a Chinese student ate with a Tibetan student, cross-cultural barriers of misunderstanding and prejudice slowly began to crack. "Living at I-House taught me more about politics than my graduate classes in political science," a student from Wisconsin told me.

Cross-cultural misunderstandings often occur during meals. In the cafeteria, different approaches to food and dining etiquette can raise eyebrows and spur spirited debate. When a visiting professor attempted to pour tea for a Korean undergraduate, she refused. Puzzled, he insisted. She explained that, in her culture, it's improper to be served by an older person with a higher status.

Sometimes strange foods or eating habits induce culture shock. When a physicist from Shanghai saw a dish labeled "turkey," he opened his dictionary and grimaced. "Turkey? That's an animal we keep in zoos." A woman from Taiwan shakes a bowl of green Jell-O; when it wiggles, she laughs. A law student from New Guinea puzzles over the box of Nut-N-Honey cereal, and a musician from Kiev studies a jar of peanut butter.

Much of the food is labeled, lest the Sri Lankan Hindu find forbidden beef in his burrito, or the Sudanese Muslim discover pork in his Thai noodles. Pleasing such a *mélange* of discriminating palates is challenging. Some students complain the food's too bland; others, that it's too spicy. Some want chopsticks; others try to adjust to not eating with their hands. Then there are special religious observances, for example, Muslim students who fast during Ramadan, and Jewish students who eat matzo during Passover. When Muslim students asked if the Jell-O was kosher, American dining room staff learned that religious Muslims and Jews couldn't eat foods made with gelatin if it came from non-kosher or non-halal animals.

The "rice question" reflects another culinary challenge of this multicultural environment. The Bhutanese like their rice red with chilies; many Indians like it with curry or yogurt; and some Iranians like yellow saffron rice with pine nuts. Some Latin Americans want rice fried with beans, while the vegetarians may want rice that is brown, organic, and with sesame seeds. Many Chinese prefer rice cooked with the grains separate and hard, while many Japanese and Thais want their grains soft and sticky.

I remember one student saying, "We never eat salad in China." During her first meal at I-House, she phoned her mother in China complaining, "They eat grass here." To make raw vegetables from the salad bar "edible," Asian students often put them in a bowl, douse them with water, and microwave them.

Once, during lunchtime in the cafeteria serving line, I was next to a Japanese resident who was looking skeptically at a "Sloppy Joe." He asked me about the strange substance inside the hamburger bun. When I told him it's a blend of ground meat, bell peppers, onions, Worcestershire sauce, ketchup, and chilies, he appeared appalled. "So unattractive," he said. "We Japanese eat with our eyes." When I reminded him of the Japanese proverb, "You can't see the whole world through a bamboo tube," he put one on his plate. We sat together and after tasting his Sloppy Joe, he called it delicious.

Like the Japanese, French students often associate the aesthetics of food with its taste. For many French students, good food should be beautifully arranged and color coordinated; to them, the eye is the opening to the appetite. The art of cooking, presenting, eating, and discussing food is central to French culture. One French Fulbright scholar observed that large American portions are a bit vulgar, because it appears that the person is more interested in filling his stomach than appreciating the beauty and delicacy of taste.

French I-House students were always intrigued whenever I brought to their attention some of the unusual ways food metaphors infuse their language. For example, *oeil au beurre noir* (an eye with black butter) means a black eye. "To be confused" is *être dans le potage* (to be in the soup). *Occupez vous de vos oignons* (mind your onions) means "to mind your own business." And *va te faire cuire un oeuf* (go cook an egg) means "go to hell"! What was their reaction to my observations? Most French never realized how often they use food references.

A challenging situation occurred when two women, both new residents from Kuwait, went to the dining room for the first time. While they were eating, they were horrified to see a dog under an adjoining table. They were upset because, for many Muslims, dogs are considered ritually unclean, and therefore aren't welcome inside homes, though they can be used outside for guarding, farming, herding, or hunting.

The two women complained to the dining manager, insisting they couldn't eat under these unclean and emotionally disturbing conditions. The manager explained that the golden retriever was not a pet, but a student's seeing-eye dog. Prisoners of their own cultural prisms, they were unmoved when the manager explained that in the U.S., the blind student is legally permitted to have his trained, canine companion with him at all times, and it is the compassionate thing to do. The Kuwaiti and American opposing beliefs were so deeply rooted, that the only immediate solution I could figure out was to have the Kuwaiti women and the blind student dine at different times, and in different sections of the large dining room—a difficult, if imperfect compromise—but one that tried to accommodate different notions of reality.

This episode reminded me of the well-known Indian legend of the blind men and the elephant. Six blind men on their way to visit the Rajah encounter an elephant. They each feel the elephant with their hands to determine what sort of creature it is. The blind man who feels a leg says the elephant is "exactly like a tree"; the one who feels the tail says the elephant is "like a rope"; the one who feels the trunk says the elephant is "like a snake"; and, the one who feels the ear says, "You are all mad! It resembles a fan in every way." The fifth, who feels the belly, says the elephant is "like a wall"; and the sixth, who feels the tusk, says, "Anyone can tell it is like a spear." Each man begins to argue his own point with such conviction that a fight starts.

Just at that point, the Rajah comes along the road and stops their quarreling. The first man says, "Let us ask the Rajah to settle the exact nature of this creature." The Rajah explains that each man has only felt a small part of a very large animal. To learn the truth, wise men must put together every small part to learn about the whole.

To Sit or Not to Sit?

Rooms in I-House don't have private bathrooms; each floor has communal toilets and showers. Several incidents made me appreciate how much toilet etiquette can vary across cultures. Louis, an I-House maintenance worker, excitedly told me that he'd just seen "the damnedest thing." While he was cleaning the showers that morning, he noticed one toilet stall door was closed for a long time. Wondering why no one came out, Louis peered under the door and didn't see any feet. He pushed on the door, but it was locked. Concerned, he assumed the toilet either was plugged up or something was broken. He entered the adjacent stall, stood on the closed toilet cover and looked over the barrier. "Joe,' he said, "I saw a student with his feet on the toilet seat crouching over the bowl. So, I leaned over and told him: 'Sit down, relax. You're in America!'"

That's when I began to realize why some students had complained about seeing footprints on the toilet seats. I looked for an explanation. I read news reports that in airport bathrooms from Tokyo to San Francisco, there were footprints on the sit-down toilet seats. At the Beijing Olympics, so many non-Chinese athletes complained about having to squat that organizers refit the toilets at three main Olympic venues. Someone showed me a sign with a drawing: "Do Not Step On The Toilet Seats." Another sign read: "Sit, Don't Squat."

More than a billion people in parts of Asia, Africa, the Middle East, and Latin America relieve themselves by crouching and straddling a hole in the floor. A growing number of medical doctors believe this traditional, natural way of relieving yourself is healthier than the modern sit-down toilet. Some now advise people: "Squat, don't sit; it's the healthy way to poop."

Those who sit on toilet seats regard the footprints as disrespectful and unhygienic; those who squat can't understand why anyone would put their butt on the same seat strangers used. How disgusting!

Are you a sitter, squatter, sprayer, splasher, or wiper? Students from Germany to Chile to Egypt have different answers. I'll never forget an Indian graduate student who complained that the most irritating thing about living in I-House was that the Western toilets weren't fitted with spray water hoses. He explained his perspective (shared by a number of Asians, Middle Easterners, and Latin Americans): "In our latrines, there's no toilet paper. Can you imagine cleaning your bottom with just pieces of paper? We use a pressurized water hose or a water tap and bucket to splash ourselves clean. You lean forward and target the desired area with water, then clear it with your left hand to clean (many people of the world eat only with their right hands!). Give yourself a minute to air dry. After the business, wash your hands with soap." He enumerated his case against toilet paper: it doesn't get you clean. It gives you a friction rash. It kills trees. It's bad for the environment and clogs the plumbing.

At an overnight retreat for new residents, a Japanese student told a female staff member that the toilet cubicles at I-House weren't completely private. "I was shocked," she confided. There are gaps between doors, and big gaps under each door. I couldn't pee. The girls waiting outside could see my feet." Many Japanese public bathrooms, she explained, have cubicle walls and doors that reach from the floor to the ceiling to ensure privacy.

That sense of privacy for the Japanese student in the toilet cubicle reminded me that most students wanted single rooms and preferred not to share them with other students. So, I was taken aback when a Nigerian graduate student who was entitled to a single room asked to be switched to a double room. When asked why, he said that he felt lonely, that he missed sharing a room with his siblings at home. Only then did I understand the Russian proverb, "The four corners of the room are the guests of the lonely man."

Questions and Activities, Chapter Two

1. At International House, with residents from about 80 countries, it's not surprising that many love affairs have developed into marriages across cultures. After the initial excitement begins to fade, these couples often face important intercultural challenges and learning opportunities.

    Interview a couple from two different countries, ethnicities or religions who have lived together for at least a year. Ask each of them to describe any cultural differences that may have caused specific misperceptions, or miscommunications in their relationship. How might cultural differences have also caused misunderstandings about gender roles, communication styles, use of language, ways of handling conflicts, food and drink, the behaviors of their respective partner's family or proper ways of raising children? What were the couple's most and least effective ways of handling these misunderstandings or conflicts?

2. The children of intercultural, inter-ethnic, interfaith or inter-racial marriages often see themselves as bicultural or bi-racial, with multiple frames of cultural reference. To learn more about those with mixed cultural identities, log on to your *Cultural Detective Online* subscription, and click on the *Blended Culture* Package. After reviewing the "Introduction to Blended Culture" page, click on the Supplementary Material tab and read, "Distinguishing Between Encapsulated and Constructive Blended Culture Experiences" and "Pathways into Blended Culture." Then, still under the Supplementary Material section, review the "Critical Incident: Blended Teamwork." After considering the first two questions of the debrief, discuss your response to the third question with your colleagues, classmates or friends.

3. Describe examples of foods and ways of eating that you might consider strange, abnormal, or perhaps even offensive. What may have caused you to have those feelings and attitudes? Ask classmates, colleagues or friends from three or four countries, preferably on at least three different continents, to see if they have similar or different reactions to your ideas about food and ways of eating. In what ways do their preferences differ, and what might these differences suggest about different values in your respective societies?

4. What was your reaction to the LGBT community's response to the Valentines' Day Poster described in Chapter 2? If you identify with the LGBT community, what, from your point of view, are some misconceptions about the LGBT community and/or you as an individual from that community? If you consider yourself to be "straight" or "cisgender," what are your feelings and questions about those who identify with the LGBT community? Do you know "straight" people who may view the LGBT community differently than you?

    To learn more about the LGBT community, log on to your *Cultural Detective Online* subscription and click on the *Lesbian, Gay, Bisexual, Transgender (LGBT)* Package. After reviewing the "Introduction" page, click on the Lenses tab and review the values for the LGBT community as a whole. Then, click on specific Values Lenses for the Lesbian, Gay, Bisexual and Transgender communities respectively. In each case, putting your cursor over a Values Lens will reveal tendencies in the LGBT community plus a possible Negative Perception from those who may not value the same things. Based on your review and discussion of these Values Lenses, proceed to the Incident tab and review "The Pride Parade," including the contrasting perceptions between the parade organizers and Peter, who identifies as straight. In what respects do you agree or disagree with the ideas presented, including proposed ways of building cultural bridges between straight and LGBT groups? Why? What might you add to these basic Author Ideas?

CHAPTER THREE

Seeing U.S. Americans
Through the Eyes of Others

"You cannot see the mountain when you are on it."
—Chinese proverb

People from other cultures can offer U.S. Americans some eye-opening observations about our common behaviors. During my UC Berkeley cross-cultural communication class for visiting business students from China, I gave an assignment to help them understand aspects of American culture: "Describe behaviors you've observed during your initial weeks in the San Francisco Bay area that seem strange or confusing—things that you've never seen at home."

The students, from various regions of China, were surprised that they hadn't seen any clotheslines. When they asked me where Americans dry their underwear, I explained that in cities people tend to use dryers, but there are more clotheslines outside urban areas. They stressed that whether or not Chinese people have dryers, they are sure to wash their underwear daily. "Do they wash them every day because they don't have enough underwear?" I asked. They assured me that, even though most Chinese have multiple pairs of underwear, each evening they wash their underwear from that day.

Puzzled, I explained that my wife and I put our underwear in a hamper with all the other dirty laundry. Each Sunday, we wash and dry all the clothes together. "Together?!" They were shocked. "Why," they asked, "would you allow your soiled underwear to get caked up for more than a day? And why would you mix your stained underwear with your shirts, blouses, and slacks?" One student from Beijing explained, "Accumulating and mixing dirty underwear is not only unhygienic, but it's also an inappropriate exposure of body secrets."

While washers and dryers are increasingly common in Chinese cities, most Chinese—especially those of the older generation—hand-wash their underwear and don't like dryers. A student from Chengdu said her mother believes that sunshine sterilizes clothes; the way to compliment clean clothes in Chinese is to compare them to "the smell of sunlight." Perhaps this explains why Western hotel staffers are sometimes baffled to find Chinese hotel guests have left their underwear drying on lampshades and windowsills.

Frequently, I hear international students and other visitors in the U.S. comment that, during initial encounters, Americans often appear warm and enthusiastic. They're surprised, intrigued, or confused by how often Americans smile at people they don't know. While a Vietnamese and a French student were walking in Golden Gate Park, a stranger on a bicycle smiled and said, "Hey! How are you?" Before they could answer, the biker sped off. "Why do Americans ask how I am and then go off without waiting for an answer?" the French student asked me. She compared Americans' casual, quick greetings to fast food— "neither have any taste or feeling." She didn't realize that, in the U.S., often the expression, "How are you?" is not a request for information but, rather, is just another way of saying hello.

U.S. American students, accustomed to having their smiles returned, often perceive unsmiling Asians as cold and unfriendly. Few Americans are aware that in many Asian cultures expressing emotion—especially with a stranger—reflects immaturity and a lack of self-control. One Chinese student explained it this way: "We Chinese are like a thermos bottle—cold outside, warm inside."

Another common U.S. American custom that makes many international students uncomfortable is the casual use of first names instead of respectful titles and the family name. In my UC Berkeley classes, and at International House, students from most countries in Africa, Asia, Europe, Latin America, and the Middle East generally felt uncomfortable calling me "Joe." Because they're from more formal and hierarchical societies than the U.S., they preferred calling me "Professor Lurie," "Director Lurie," or "Mister Lurie."

When Americans say, "call me by my first name," often we are signaling our "we're all the same" egalitarian value. But some visitors may find this informality disrespectful and insensitive to rank and age. Students from Guatemala to Ghana, and other societies in which group and family interests take precedence over those of the individual, are unable to call me by my first name. Many simply call me "Lurie."

To my ears, "Lurie" once sounded disrespectful. That was until I realized that when people from many Asian and African countries address me this way, they're showing respect for my family, age, and role in society. Recently, a former UC student from Zambia sent me an email that began, "Dear Mr. Joe." Like her, a number of students can't completely disengage from the patterns and values of their home societies, so I've gotten used to being called "Mr. Joe." In time though, some students did become comfortable enough to just call me "Joe."

Feeling comfortable with another name is one thing, but adjusting to an unexpected request from the opposite sex is quite another. A former assistant in my office related that, after her cousin left Beijing, he obtained a job as a waiter in a suburban New York Chinese restaurant. Once, when he served a "round-eye" woman (e.g., Caucasian), the customer told him, "You're real cute." He was dumbfounded. As she left the restaurant, she slipped him a note: "If you're not married, I'd like to see you again." On it was her cell number. He didn't know what to do, but took a risk and phoned, apologizing for having little money and no car. Unperturbed, she boldly offered to pick him up in her car.

To many international students, even more striking than an American female asking a male stranger for a date, is the profound gulf that separates many U.S. American youth from the elderly. "I find America is so youth-obsessed," a Taiwanese psychology student observed. "I see TV ads encouraging women in their 40s and 50s to have facelifts. I see mothers dressing like their daughters. It seems many Americans feel insulted if they're called 'old' because they think it means 'useless.' We attach more importance to age. To us, the word 'old' implies respect. When an American friend told me he took his father on a trip as a birthday gift, I was surprised. For most Taiwanese a trip together isn't a gift, it's a duty."

Students from many parts of the world are surprised that so many young U.S. Americans want to live on their own during and after college (if they have a job). In many other countries, college students live with their parents after graduation, and depend on them financially until they marry. A Jordanian student explained to me the importance of mutual dependence and obligation—caring for parents as they have cared for their children—this way: "Eventually, we become our parents' retirement plan.'

A Korean student, whose parents care for her grandparents in their apartment near Seoul, was astonished to learn that many elderly Americans live separately from their children— sometimes thousands of miles away in retirement and nursing homes. "I don't understand how American elders can say, 'I don't want to be a burden to my children,' or 'I want to keep my independent life.' It must pain them to feel their children are too busy to care for them. It must be so lonely."

Like her, many people from traditional Asian, African, Middle Eastern, and Latin American extended families also have trouble understanding our strong spirit of individualism. When four graduate students—a Brazilian, two Ethiopians, and a U.S. American—finished eating at a popular pizzeria, the American took the bill and examined it carefully. "He asked how many beers each of us consumed, did the math, and then told each of us how much to pay," the Ethiopian woman complained. "For all three of us, seeing him splitting our bill was strange and offensive." In many countries, where mutual dependence and obligation are normal, one person pays for the meal; the next time, someone else reciprocates. "Every man for himself," is a peculiar U.S. American concept for many people around the world.

My American students were surprised to hear Keiko, a graduate student from Osaka, admit she had to abandon her dream of becoming a journalist. To respect her parents' wishes, she was studying engineering, because it is more secure financially. She then startled the Americans further when she described the mothers in her Oakland apartment building. "I can't believe they ask their children, 'What do you want to eat? What do you want to wear today? Do you want to watch Netflix or play with Legos?' American parents encourage their children to make so many independent choices." Keiko went on to explain that giving children so much independence could encourage excessive arguments and divisions within a family.

Stanley, a computer science graduate student from Texas, said that he'd never considered the possible downsides of individualism that Keiko pointed out. He stressed that choice, risk-taking, and even challenging authority help explain American entrepreneurship and invention. Keiko granted that she had not fully realized the possible upsides of individualism, until Stanley pointed out that some places, like Silicon Valley, might value flexibility, innovation, and questioning those in power.

***

> *"Everything that irritates us about others can lead us to an understanding of ourselves."*
> —Carl Jung

While a U.S. American professor, his Chinese wife, and their infant were living with her family in China, he discovered that many Chinese have a very different relationship with privacy than Westerners do. As he wrote in his amusing and revealing blog post, "American Anxieties and Chinese Secrets," in *Becoming Chinese*, "My mother-in-law entered my bedroom, the most private of all rooms, and rummaged through that most private of all places—my underwear drawer."

"How do I know she did this? Upon returning from work, I found her with a pile of half my underwear on the kitchen table, a pair of scissors in her hand, and the other half of my underwear cut to shreds on the floor. Needless to say, I was mortified that my mother-in-law had not only seen my underwear but was also touching them, carefully selecting the cleanest parts of the fabrics to cut out and throwing away the rest. With such intimate knowledge of my most private pieces of clothing, I was certain she'd never look at me the same again."

He went on to point out that, "she had good intentions, even if her actions left me in need of new underwear and a therapist. Alarmed at the damage to my son's skin that would ensue from the plastic diapers we uncaring Americans use, she intended to fashion my son some more skin-friendly, homemade cloth diapers from my undergarments."

Chu-hua, a student in one of my UC Berkeley intercultural communication classes, explained that in Mandarin, the word for "privacy" roughly translates as "selfish" or "hidden," concepts that are not conducive to communal living and family unity. Chu-hua pointed out that in an American-Chinese marriage, often the American marries the entire Chinese family. The relatives may visit frequently, and for weeks at a time, oblivious to the American's sense of boundaries. For example, a Chinese father-in-law might enter the bathroom while his stunned American son-in-law is on the toilet. The American husband might describe this loss of privacy as "an invasion." The Chinese relatives don't understand such "odd" Western notions of privacy.

My wife and I learned a lot about privacy when Mei, a Chinese patent attorney, studying for her PhD at UC Berkeley, asked if she could bring her parents to our home to experience a "typical" American-style dinner. This was their first time outside of China. Upon arrival, they wandered from room to room, taking photos of our bookcases, our treadmill, our shower, and our toilet. We pretended we weren't offended, but we felt violated. Mei had requested we prepare an "authentic" American dinner. Our menu included a thick New York steak, ketchup, fries, and raw vegetable salad with Thousand Island dressing. As eating the steak with forks and knives was such a struggle, we finally gave them chopsticks. Still, they didn't eat most of the steak or salad. And the apple pie? They barely tasted it.

To our surprise, her mother and father said something in Mandarin and then went to our kitchen and unpacked two grocery bags they'd brought, filled with Chinese ingredients. We were stunned as they rummaged through our refrigerator and shelves searching for soy sauce, sugar, and chilies. Where was our rice cooker? My wife and I felt our privacy being violated. They were frustrated that we didn't have a wok and exasperated by our useless electric cooktop. How could anyone cook without a natural flame? They prepared a second dinner: superb spicy Hunan-style dishes. Nothing was more natural to them than treating their daughter's American friends' home almost as if it were their own.

We had more dining adventures when my wife and I were invited to a dinner party with a group of administrators visiting from the University of Pau, in southwest France. We were the only non-French included. Looking out from the table, the French visitors marveled at the red-streaked sunset over San Francisco. Claudette, the French woman on my right, served me an ample portion of coq au vin and filled my glass with Merlot. I took the platter and served the woman on my left. I glanced across the table at my wife. As the man on her left was about to place a generous portion of coq au vin on her plate, she motioned him to stop. "I had a big lunch," she announced, "so, if you don't mind, I'll serve myself." And assuming the French man on her right would wish to serve himself, my wife passed him the platter instead of serving him, as is normal in France.

The French seemed stunned by her lack of etiquette. Having lived and worked in France for four years, I understood their confusion by what they perceived as my wife's American impoliteness. During the meal, I explained that the American way of serving ourselves might seem rude or selfish to them, but it reflects our individualism, that we want to determine for ourselves how much and what food we want. I explained that when Americans say, "help yourself," they're giving their guests freedom of choice, unaware that this expression might sound rude to people from cultures where it's inappropriate to serve yourself. The French visitors nodded understandingly when I told them a Japanese friend says the expression "help yourself" makes him feel unwelcome, as if no one was willing to help him.

My remarks opened up a frank cross-cultural discussion about French perceptions and misperceptions about U.S. Americans. A French woman told me when she saw her bill for lunch in a Napa Valley restaurant, she felt angry. "In France, the bill is exactly what the menu says, with the tax and tip built-in. In America, the bill is deceptive, much higher than the menu price. They add several taxes, and the waiters expect at least a fifteen-to-twenty percent tip. To me, Americans are trying to make money any way they can. It's greedy." Through the French prism, American waiters seem falsely attentive, trying to solicit a large tip, yet they want customers to leave quickly so they can get more customers and more tips.

In France, waiters generally don't bring the bill until customers request it. From a U.S. American perspective, they're not eager for customers to leave because their tips already are part of the bill and are shared with all the waiters. And, perhaps, some waiters don't want to encourage more table turnover, because it means more work.

In other dining misperceptions, Neha, an Indian filmmaker engaged to an Italian-American, told me that her soon-to-be mother-in-law complains that she and her Indian friends eat with their hands. "She calls it unsanitary, which is so silly. Americans eat sandwiches and cookies and chips with their hands." Neha jolted my own unconscious assumptions about hygiene when she asked me, "What do you think is cleaner, eating with your hand or with a fork in a restaurant? When I answered, "a fork," she disagreed. "I don't know how well the restaurant washed the fork, but I know I washed my hands!"

***

"Every tongue, every nation, has its own vibration."
—Jamaican proverb

Since 2008, I've been coaching new immigrant professionals, from Bolivia to Iran to Ukraine, focusing on how to search for work in the U.S. Our discussions about résumés, cover letters, interviewing, and the American workplace provide an intriguing array of insights into life in the U.S. As always, there are plenty of mutual misinterpretations. For example, while a Burmese man was interviewing for a job in Silicon Valley as a software engineer, the U.S. American interviewer asked him, "How do you deal with stress?" The Burmese job seeker answered, "I take a nap." This response may be acceptable in some contexts, but not in an American job interview.

The highly-skilled immigrants I work with often give me valuable cross-cultural knowledge, which is useful when I train their American mentors—volunteers from companies ranging from Google to Facebook to Wells Fargo—to understand the behaviors and values they may find confusing. Many of these immigrants are from countries where modesty and unpretentiousness are extremely valued, as illustrated by the Chinese proverb, "You cannot propel yourself forward by patting yourself on the back." The proverb's message clashes with some key qualities that can help job seekers in the U.S. stand out: accomplishments and self-promotion.

In some of my training sessions, I run mock interviews. When I ask interviewees to look me in the eye and speak confidently about how their skills can be an asset to the company, some have great difficulty. To demonstrate, I asked a Filipino job seeker, in his late-thirties, to tell me about his professional experience. He averted his eyes and responded, "I'm just a doctor."

"What kind of doctor?" I questioned.

"I do a little of everything," he said softly.

Searching for some specifics, I asked if he'd ever performed any surgery.

"A little bit," he offered shyly.

I persisted. "Have you ever done heart surgery or had experience with organ transplants?"

"Yes, a bit of both," he responded self-effacingly.

After more probing, I discovered that this unpretentious man had been one of the most respected surgeons in the Philippines, and the director of a major clinic.

Amita was an unassuming Nepalese immigrant working as a sales clerk at Macy's. During a coaching session, I noticed on her résumé that she'd been a television anchor in Kathmandu. I suggested she strengthen her résumé by adding a section called, "Awards and Special Accomplishments," and asked what she might write in it.

Amita looked uncomfortable and said she couldn't think of anything in particular. Noticing she'd studied at Johns Hopkins University for a year, I asked how she'd financed her education. "I received a bit of financial aid," she said humbly. After I pressed her for additional information, she reluctantly revealed that she'd been awarded a full fellowship plus a stipend.

Sensing that her résumé didn't disclose the extent of her accomplishments, I asked if she'd ever received any other awards. Amita hesitated, and then said yes. This was my clue that, under her reserve and humility, this unassertive woman was hiding something significant. What kind of award? With averted eyes, she admitted that the then-King of Nepal had given her a medal for noteworthy service.

"What kind of service?" I pushed. Reluctantly, Amita revealed that she'd been selected to host both Hillary Clinton and Prince Charles during their visits to Nepal. With some more probing, she added that she was the King's interpreter during his discussions with Colin Powell.

I told her that putting these three accomplishments on her résumé could improve her chances of securing job interviews. However, because of her deeply ingrained cultural sense of modesty, she only listed one or two of these achievements.

***

"He who boasts of his accomplishments will reap ridicule."
—Filipino proverb

"He whose face gives no light shall never become a star."
—William Blake

U.S. American recruiters and employers commonly ask during interviews, "What was your most important accomplishment?" Job seekers from countries as varied as Laos, Bolivia, and Madagascar usually answer with "we" rather than "I." During a practice interview, I posed this question to Mwamba, an electrical engineer from Tanzania. He answered, "We were able to design a system that was used throughout the country." When I asked him to identify his role in the project, he kept reverting to "we," explaining that his accomplishments depended on others. Mwamba's parents—like those of many immigrants coming from cultures that value strong extended families—discouraged him from using the word "I."

Job seekers from strong extended families also have a revealing way of responding to a typical U.S. American opening interview question: "Tell me about yourself." For example, during an interview for a biotech position, Boon-nam, a soft-spoken Thai, responded by describing his parents; his sister, a professor at Chulalongkorn University; and his uncle, the head monk in a temple near Bangkok.

When Boon-nam asked me why the American interviewer seemed impatient with his answers and kept asking him to speak more loudly, I explained that many Americans consider a soft, self-effacing voice and a gentle handshake to be signs of weakness. But in Thailand, as in many other cultures, a raised voice and firm handshake are perceived as aggressive and unrefined.

It is not easy for non-Western job seekers like Boon-nam to understand that when faced with a "tell me about yourself" interview-opening question, they are expected to focus on how well their skills and accomplishments align with the job requirements, and not discuss their family backgrounds and connections. For many non-Western immigrants to land a job, family connections are far more significant than they are in the U.S. Even though a relative or friend's referral can help open an American employer's doors, the prevailing value in the U.S. is that an individual's talents, experience, and accomplishments are what really matter.

When I explained to Omar, who was an accountant in Baghdad, that, in the U.S., getting a job using family connections is generally considered unethical and a conflict of interest, he made me think about "nepotism" in a different light. Omar said that when he graduated university in Baghdad, his cousin hired him. "He knew I had the right skills and he trusts me. He's known me since I was born." This method, insisted Omar, is far more efficient than interviewing many strangers who might have inflated résumés and candy-coated referrals. While I still believe fair job competition should be based on a candidate's demonstrated experience and skills, I had to admit that Omar had a point.

***

"When you shoot an arrow of truth, dip its point in honey."
—Arab proverb

A year after I helped Ayaka, originally from Osaka, Japan, obtain a job with a computer-game company's marketing department, she contacted me. Although she said she enjoyed her demanding job, she found many of her American colleagues unnecessarily direct and frank. Coming from a culture where preserving another person's dignity and maintaining good personal relations is very important, Ayaka was offended when a co-worker openly challenged her marketing ideas in front of other colleagues.

Ayaka was often shaken by her co-workers' directness. For example, when she asked, "Can we review the agenda?" her co-worker replied curtly, "No, I don't have time now." In the Japanese workplace, people aren't so direct and confrontational, Ayaka explained. "In Japan, the response might be, 'Please let me think about that.' Japanese know that sentence means 'No.'" This behavior reminded me of the wonderful book, *Sixteen Ways to Avoid Saying 'No.'* Author Masaaki Imai explains that one way to say "no" in Japanese is to say "yes." It's not surprising that another of his books is titled, *Never Take Yes for an Answer.*

Ayaka described how disagreements or negative feedback are handled in the Japanese workplace, in a much different and more indirect manner than in the U.S. For example, a U.S. American might say, "That idea won't work." A Japanese might be subtler, as in, "What an interesting idea. Are there perhaps other approaches we might consider?"

During her performance evaluation, Ayaka's supervisor's negative comments shocked and hurt her. She said he pointed out that her assistant often was late to work and dressed sloppily. "He criticized me for not managing her properly. Instead of telling me I was a poor manager, why didn't he say, 'Your assistant is perhaps not very well these days.' I would have understood that comment, instead of feeling attacked."

When I asked Ayaka how she would speak to a Japanese employee who was regularly late to work, she answered, "I'd simply ask, 'How are you?' She'd know exactly what I meant."

In Japan, as in many Asian countries, it's desirable to carefully avoid offensive comments, and mask negative feelings and intentions. Instead of direct orders to subordinates, Japanese might carefully use subtle, vague words, euphemisms, facial expressions, or prolonged silences. Ayaka gave me a deeper understanding about why American-directness can make some newcomers to the U.S. think we're unrefined and impolite. And conversely, if Americans don't understand the nuances of indirect communication, they may feel frustrated and regard some Asian behaviors as "inscrutable" or even "deceptive."

***

"The eye sees only what the mind is prepared to comprehend."
—Henry-Louis Bergson

During a class observation assignment, Dorjee, a student from Tibet, ventured into San Francisco. "I saw many elderly people walking by themselves. It's shocking," he reported to my class. "In Tibet, I never saw an old person walking alone. It's difficult for me to understand why Americans value self-reliance so much. Many times, I feel alone, not because Americans aren't caring, but because many times they like doing things on their own." He described a student camping trip to Yosemite. "On the bus, we had fun talking and laughing. When we arrived, I thought our group always would go hiking together, eat together. We didn't. A lot of the Americans went off to swim, sleep, or play the guitar. I don't understand this idea of 'Do your own thing.' People like me, who are used to group activities, felt lost."

I led a seminar on U.S. American culture for visiting South Korean journalists and asked them to share perceptions of American behaviors they'd encountered. Many said they were surprised to see people sitting alone, eating alone, and even going to the movies alone. They wondered if these people were "mentally disturbed." Their observations made me reflect on how the U.S. American spirit of individualism could be liberating, yet also can lead to isolation. And I began to understand why many Korean, Chinese, Japanese, and Thai tourists prefer to travel in groups. If given "free time" to explore a city on their own, instead of welcoming it, they may feel confused and unhappy.

A Korean newspaper editor spent an afternoon at Fisherman's Wharf in San Francisco, and was astonished to see a black man, his Caucasian wife, and their bi-racial children eating at a picnic table. "No one stared at them disapprovingly," he told the class. "In Korea, 'mixing blood' is a disgrace and a dishonor to the family."

Sensing that the Korean visitors might think interracial couples are very common in the U.S., I pointed out that in many places these couples still are frowned upon, even shunned. The editor went on to describe seeing a Caucasian couple pushing a stroller. "The baby was Asian!" Among Koreans, the issue of "parental blood" is so important, he added, that when a Korean couple adopts a Korean child, sometimes the wife pretends she's pregnant to maintain family dignity.

His comments prompted another Korean journalist to add that with globalization, the number of inter-ethnic couples is increasing very gradually in Korea, but they're not easily accepted.

A Korean radio reporter was surprised to observe many American women, men, and children openly sporting tattoos. Tattoos are associated with gangsters in Korea, she explained. Men with tattoos were forbidden from serving in the military (serious, because if you're not good enough to serve and protect the country, employers often discriminate against you). Today, the Korean military allows tattoos, but only if they're hidden. They're officially illegal unless given by a licensed doctor, but many young people are now getting tattoos at illegal underground "tat" studios—as a form of social rebellion.

***

"Every tale can be told in a different way."
—Greek proverb

When another Korean journalist took BART (the subway) to San Francisco, he noticed several passengers put their feet on empty seats. "Why," he asked, "Would anyone want to sit where someone had placed his dirty shoes?" In Korea, Thailand, some other Asian countries, and in much of the Middle East, crossing the feet and exposing the sole of a shoe or foot is offensive. When sitting with elders, Koreans are expected to show respect by planting both feet on the floor.

During their travels through the San Francisco Bay area, the Korean journalists also were surprised to see some men without shirts, and women breastfeeding in public.

Their shock at public displays of flesh reminded me of the time when a sixty-two-year-old author friend from Beijing visited my home. When she noticed a Modigliani print of a nude woman in my living room, she averted her eyes nervously. When I asked why, she explained that in China, displays of nudity in public or in a home are not appreciated. During her next visit, she laughed when she saw that I had covered the Modigliani picture with a towel.

During a class for French and Chinese business students, we studied how ads could reveal cultural values. Each student showed an ad from his or her country and explained why it was successful. One French student showed a provocative magazine ad for a perfume: a gorgeous, voluptuous blonde wearing nothing above her waist but a skimpy black bra. Most French students called the provocative ad "classy" or "appealing"; most Chinese students deemed it "offensive" or "unpleasant."

The discussion caused us to think about nudity in new ways. While pornography in the U.S. is easily accessible, and, though there are niche nudist colonies and beaches, outright public nudity is not condoned. Most U.S. Americans are surprised, and often shocked, when they see bare-breasted women on many French, Italian, Spanish, and German beaches. Francoise, a marketing student in my class, said that French lipstick ads with images of bare-breasted mermaids flopped in the U.S.

We then discussed the story of Starbucks, which sparked controversy in the U.S., not about café latte, but about anatomy. In 2008, it reintroduced an old logo, featuring a topless two-tailed mermaid who is supposed to be as seductive as coffee itself, and who symbolizes the seafaring history of coffee. A small, fringe Christian group protesting the "offensive" mermaid called for a national boycott of the coffee-selling giant, dubbing it "Slutbucks." It nabbed media attention from the U.S. to the UK to Pakistan. A Washington school district banned Starbucks coffee unless drinkers concealed the seductive mermaid's breasts with a cup holder. In the redesign, Starbucks "cleaned up" the logo: the mermaid's lengthened hair now drapes over her breasts.

My understanding about what we see, and what we don't, were shaken when an Indian post-doctoral research scholar at UC Berkeley invited me for lunch one day. He was relocating for a new job, and wanted to show appreciation for my hospitality, so he gave me a beautifully wrapped gift. As in many countries, he respectfully gave it to me with both hands. Similarly, I expressed respect by receiving it with my two hands. Aware that people in many countries often do not open gifts in front of the givers, I hesitated and thanked him. As I was about to put the unwrapped gift into my briefcase, he insisted, "Go ahead, Mr. Joe, open it." He'd been living in the U.S. long enough to know that most Americans enjoy opening gifts in front of the giver.

He eagerly watched as I opened it. It was a portrait of a greying bearded man.

Impressed, I said, "What a stunning portrait of Sigmund Freud!" His expectant face suddenly changed. He looked disappointed. I realized that my perception of the portrait was horribly wrong. Remembering the connection between his background and his love of Indian literature, I quickly corrected myself: "What a striking portrait of Rabindranath Tagore!" (a great Bengali writer and Nobel Laureate).

It was a great relief that we ended up recognizing the same bearded man. This uncomfortable moment made me appreciate why in so many cultures people often open gifts in private—in case the gift is disappointing, they avoid mutual embarrassment.

But why did I initially see Sigmund Freud? Perhaps because I'd recently visited the Freud Museum in Vienna, and had seen an array of photos of the bearded Freud in his later years?

In my classes, I sometimes show the portrait of the bearded man to students and ask who he is. Their answers range wildly, from Da Vinci to Tolstoy to Plato. Each student's interests and experiences color his or her perceptions. Several times, when the students can't associate the face with anything familiar, the answer is, "It's you, Mr. Joe!"

Questions and Activities, Chapter Three

1. Interview a recent immigrant or exchange student about their experiences in your country. What have they seen and/or experienced that seemed strange, confusing, perhaps even shocking—things they never saw or experienced in their own country? What might these reactions reveal about their personal and cultural values? In what ways may these perceptions have caused you to look at your own culture in different ways?

2. To deepen your understanding of mainstream culture in the United States, log on to your *Cultural Detective Online* subscription and click on the *USA* Package. After reviewing the "Introduction," click on the Values Lens for perspectives on U.S. American mainstream values. Hover your cursor over each of the values for what they may mean in U.S. American society and click to consider the possible Negative Perceptions from other points of view. How do you see these values playing out in U.S. American culture? Have you experienced some of the examples described? Have you shared any of the Negative Perceptions? What beliefs and values might you see demonstrated in U.S. society that are not reflected in the Values Lens? Compare your answers with U.S. American and international friends, classmates or colleagues.

3. Select a print, web and/or YouTube advertisement from the USA, and explain how the product, selection of words, images and colors used in the ad reflect the country's prominent mainstream cultural values, preferences and behaviors. After explaining the reason you think the ad is effective in the United States, ask others from different countries why the ad's product, use of words, images and colors would or would not be effective in their countries. What do their responses suggest about values and cultural differences in their countries? How might their responses explain their perceptions or misperceptions of life in the United States?

4. For an understanding of specific cultural contrasts with mainstream U.S. American culture, return to your *Cultural Detective Online* subscription, *USA* Package. Click on the Incidents tab and go to the story entitled, "Informal Barbecue." Read the story and complete the Worksheet, describing the Words and Actions of both the U.S. American and Taiwanese engineers. Note also what similar or contrasting values and beliefs you think are reflected in their respective approaches in the incident. Compare your response to the Author Ideas. How do the contrasting values and beliefs of those in the story compare and contrast with your own? Compare your analysis and responses with classmates, colleagues or friends from other cultures.

CHAPTER FOUR

Words That Conceal, Words That Reveal

*"Words, like eyeglasses, blur everything
that they do not make clear."*
—Joseph Joubert

Sally Lewis was recently retired from teaching English at an Ivy League college when she moved from Boston to San Francisco. She confided that she had few friends and felt isolated. Her qualifications were excellent, so I hired her to help with a writing project. Grateful, she accepted. After working together for one month, I phoned and asked when we could meet to discuss the last phase of her work.

"I don't know, Joe," she replied abruptly. "My calendar is packed."

Packed? She'd told me she was lonely. Worried about our approaching deadline, I assumed she was putting me off because she hadn't finished editing. Early the next morning, she phoned.

"Sorry, I couldn't respond yesterday," she said sweetly. "I was exhausted. I'd just flown back from Boston, and my calendar was packed somewhere in my suitcase."

Within our own culture, words often mean different things depending on the context. Imagine how much more frequently words are confusing across cultures.

***

*"If two languages say the same thing,
it is not the same thing."*
—Roman proverb

George, a graduate student in physics from Illinois, told me that his new Chinese roommate asked him, "Have you eaten?"

"Not yet," George responded. "Will you join me for lunch?"

"No, thanks," the Chinese student said. "I've already eaten." And then he walked away.

Confused about his roommate's invitation and subsequent strange behavior, George reported it to an American woman who'd studied in Beijing. She solved the enigma. George's roommate had translated the Chinese expression literally: *nǐ chīfàn le ma* (你吃饭了吗) "You eat meal yet?"

It wasn't an invitation to have a meal together, but rather a common Chinese greeting which means, "How are you?" or "Are you okay?" And, of course, if you haven't eaten, you're probably hungry and not okay.

Even if, technically, you speak the same language (for example, English), a word can have different meanings for different people. One evening, the American front desk receptionist at I-House overheard a resident from London tell a woman, "I'll come to your room later and knock you up." The receptionist was startled, unaware that in the British Commonwealth, the expression means "to waken" or "to knock on a door." Another time, she was perplexed when a male resident from Australia asked if she had "a rubber." How was she to know he meant an eraser, not a condom?

A visiting scholar from Oxford told me that he was confused when an American professor decided to "table" a controversial issue during a meeting. He couldn't understand why the matter was dropped, because in the UK, to "table" an issue means to discuss it.

Another example of how words may not be translated accurately within or across languages occurred at my farewell retirement party from International House. Before it started, a Kenyan resident greeted me effusively, saying she was looking forward to the "barbeque." I thought she was teasing me about all the playful and satiric criticism I expected to receive that evening.

As we walked into the auditorium, she looked around quizzically as students, staff, and alumni took their seats for my "Roast and Toast." "When will they serve dinner?" she asked. That's when I remembered all the "roasts" I'd enjoyed in Kenya...but roasts of a different, cross-cultural kind.

When a Pakistani-American friend returned to California with his new bride, a dental hygienist, I offered to help "Americanize" her résumé. During our first phone coaching session, I pointed out that three sentences needed a period. She fell silent; I didn't know why. Perhaps she was embarrassed that her résumé wasn't professional? Or too embarrassed to say, "I don't understand," because I'd specifically told her where to put the periods? Then I remembered that Pakistanis learn British English, so I suggested she use "full stops" after the sentences. In American English, "period" is the equivalent of "full stop" in British English. "Oh, now I understand what you mean," she said, sounding relieved.

I told this story in one of my cross-cultural communication seminars for new immigrants from several countries. Hassan, a religious Muslim from Egypt, offered his interpretation: "She responded with silence because it's not appropriate in our religion to refer to menstruation, especially when talking to a man outside the family." The Egyptian saw the word through his religious prism, since both he and the Pakistani are Muslims. But the Pakistani dental hygienist was confused by the word "period," because it had no meaning in the context of our discussion about her résumé.

During the same seminar, a Sri Lankan accountant related that after she'd told her American boss a funny story, he responded: "Oh, get out!" The Sri Lankan accountant was shocked. Why was her boss ordering her to leave the room? Had she offended him? But then, sensing the American wasn't angry, she asked him what "Oh, get out" means. She was relieved when he said it merely means, "you must be kidding," or that her story was too funny to be true.

***

"The limits of my language mean the limits of my world."
—Ludwig Wittgenstein

One semester, I often drove a Nigerian, Ibo-speaking, history professor to the University of San Francisco's Fromm Institute, where we both taught. During our conversations, he'd often call me "dear." I was puzzled. I knew his wife. He knew mine. Frankly, I felt uncomfortable. Near the end of the semester, I picked him up at his house. He hopped into my car and greeted me with "Good morning, my dear." I couldn't take it anymore. "What does the word 'dear' imply when translated into Ibo?" I asked him tactfully. Understanding my confusion and unease, he laughed and explained that among Ibo men, "dear" indicates respect and friendship.

***

"I know you believe you understand what you think I said. But I am not sure you realize that what you heard is not what I meant."
—Anonymous

During one of my UC Berkeley cross-cultural classes, we were discussing cultural generalizations and national stereotypes, when Lily, a student from Shanghai, said with a smile: "We Chinese are cheap." Cheap? The American and European students were surprised that she could be so proud about this trait. Why did she cavalierly use a word that seemingly degraded and stereotyped her fellow citizens? Suspecting that the word "cheap" didn't accurately translate the idea she intended, I asked her for the Mandarin equivalent of "cheap" and its connotations or meaning in a Chinese context. Lily pointed out that "cheap" can have a positive connotation, as in "thrifty," a trait many Chinese admire.

The students were stumped. "Cheap" is admirable? To our ears, "cheap" suggests "tight wad" and "selfish," perpetuating an unfortunate, ill-informed understanding of Chinese culture. "There's nothing wrong with being careful with your money," Lily insisted. "Whenever light bulbs are on sale, my parents rush to the store to stock up. They're proud of being thrifty and spending wisely." For Lily and many other Asians, good money management and saving for the future are commendable. These are parts of Confucian values: being wise about spending, saving for a better life, avoiding debt, and caring for your family's welfare.

Recently, Marianne, a French friend, sent me an email that began with *"Coucou."* She's calling me crazy? I was surprised. Maybe her peculiar greeting was meant to be light-hearted and she'd merely misspelled cuckoo. But she's much younger. Why would she call me cuckoo? After she sent me several emails with the same odd greeting, I decided to ask. Marianne explained that *"coucou"* is an informal, friendly way of saying hello in French.

Sometimes dictionaries don't accurately translate ancient words into modern concepts. An Israeli student, proudly and with great passion, showed me his essay, written in English, about the history of women's liberation. I read, "Women want to burn the waist coat!" "Women demand free droppings!" and was baffled.

It turns out that Hebrew served mostly as a language of liturgy and literature for 2,000 years of exile, and only in the late 19th century was Hebrew revived as a living spoken language. Modern Hebrew uses ancient words for many modern concepts. "Waist coat" means "bra," and "droppings" means "abortions." He had used a dictionary to help him translate key words as he wrote his essay. When one language is translated literally word-for-word into another language, humorous, or even serious, miscommunication may occur.

A Scotsman visiting Japan got along extremely well with his Japanese host. After a couple of weeks, their friendship grew so close that the Japanese man told the Scotsman, "I would like to sleep with you." As it turned out, the Japanese host had paid him the highest compliment, which indicated total trust. A sleeping person is easy to kill because he can't defend himself. [Story from *Cross-Cultural Training Across the Individualism-Collectivism Divide*, by Harry Triandis and Richard Brislin.]

***

"England and America are two countries divided by a common language."
—George Bernard Shaw

When Nathaniel, an orthopedic surgeon from the United Kingdom, visited our house, he looked around the living room and announced, "Your house is so homely." My wife and I were startled. Unattractive? We thought maybe he'd mispronounced "homey." Later, we discovered that in British English, "homely" means cozy.

During my travels in England, I discovered other examples of one word having different meanings. I was enjoying a long evening with an uproarious journalist friend in a London pub. Out of nowhere, he announced: "I'm pissed." Pissed? I was puzzled. Why was he angry? As he downed another pint of Guinness, he became even more ribald. I didn't need a British English dictionary to realize that "pissed," means "drunk." I also heard the expression "bombed," which I assumed also meant drunk. But to the contrary, in British English, "to bomb" means to succeed.

Other well-fortified pub conversations were also eye-opening. I heard about a U.S. American exchange student who flirted with a woman at the bar. "Hi, I'm Randy," he said. "What's your name?" She slapped him. Why was she so offended? In Britain, "randy" means "horny."

Comparing American and British approaches to healthcare, my British journalist friend called the American health and pension "schemes" inefficient and needlessly expensive. In Britain, the word "scheme," doesn't mean shady or deceptive; it's simply another word for "plan."

When I visited Dublin, Sean, a former UC student, invited me to "dinner." He told me to arrive around noon. Noon? Then I realized that in Ireland, "dinner" means what I think of as lunch. He assured me we'd be having some "crack" together. Rather presumptive, a heavy drug invitation from a former student, I thought. When I told Sean that I don't do drugs, he exploded with laughter. In Irish English, "crack" or "*craic*" means having a good time.

I was doubly confused when a professor at the University of London referred to several colleagues as "crackers." Why is the University of London employing racist American whites, I wondered? My friend snickered at my ignorance, explaining that in Great Britain, "crackers" is slang for crazy.

***

"A whisper is louder than a shout."
—Filipino proverb

While the meaning of the same word many vary dramatically across cultures, the same words may convey different messages depending on whether the culture of the speaker values overstatement, understatement, or a blunt communication style.

An article in *The Economist* ["Euphemistically Speaking," May 27, 2011] described a guide to help plainspoken

Dutch executives understand their understated British colleagues. Here are four examples that also could help U.S. Americans and people from other blunt-speaking cultures:

What the British say: "I hear what you said."
What the British mean: "I disagree and do not wish to discuss it any further."
What is understood: "He accepts my point of view."

What the British say: "That's not bad."
What the British mean: "That's good or very good."
What is understood: "That's poor or mediocre."

What the British say: "I was a bit disappointed that..."
What the British mean: "I am most upset..."
What is understood: "It really doesn't matter."

What the British say: "That is an original point of view."
What the British mean: "You must be mad or very silly."
What is understood: "They like my ideas."

Other startling examples of British understatement referenced by anthropologist Kate Fox in her superb book, *Watching the English*, include a debilitating and painful chronic illness described as "a bit of a nuisance"; a truly horrific experience as "well, not exactly what I would have chosen"; an abominable act of cruelty as "not very pretty"; a sight of breathtaking beauty as "quite pretty"; and an outstanding performance or achievement as "not bad." So, it's not surprising that many Brits, who think something is merely okay, are confused when Americans refer to it as "great," "awesome," or "fabulous."

The preponderance of U.S. American marketing words such as "new," "improved," "fast," "easy," "free," and "young" are a reflection of some key American values. "New" is so important that American marketers tend to use euphemisms to avoid any suggestion of age. Today, "used cars" are called "pre-owned," which gives them a fresh luster. When the true significance of "pre-owned" begins to be associated with age, perhaps marketers will call a used car "experienced." I once saw a billboard next to a Los Angeles cemetery that said, "Come Alive! You're in the Pepsi Generation!"

***

"It's not what you tell them; it's what they hear."
—Red Auerbach

When I shared some examples of British understatement with my friend Maysoon, a Baghdad-born Arabic professor, she often couldn't understand me; she just didn't "get it." Many Westerners, she noted, are confused by the common practice in Arabic of using repetition and exaggeration to make a point, and to confirm that what is being said is true, and to be taken seriously. For example, if an Arabic-speaking woman sees a beautiful baby, she might say: "So gorgeous, it makes me insane!" Or, if she hasn't eaten lunch, she might say, "I'm dying of hunger." If she spots someone she dislikes, she might say, "George makes me want to vomit!" To express irritation, such as someone not returning a loan on time, an Arabic-speaker might say: "May God's curse fall upon you!"

Not only does the content of communication vary across cultures, but so does appropriate volume. The first time I visited Greece, I was eating in a crowded outdoor café, and everyone around me was yelling at each other. "Why are people so angry? Why are they arguing?" I asked the waiter. "They're not arguing," he explained. "They're just discussing."

I often saw the contrast in styles of expression in the relationship between David, a U.S. American, and his Israeli wife, Tamar. She, like many Israelis, is inept at small talk, and rarely softens her sentences with phrases like "Perhaps you might consider..." or "If you wouldn't mind." My wife and I were driving them back from a wine-tasting trip in the Napa Valley. As we neared fog-shrouded San Francisco, the sun disappeared. "Oh God," Tamar moaned, "We're entering the heart of darkness!"

Another time, during dinner at their house, Tamar felt chilly. "Turn up the heat," she told David. "I don't want to live like a character out of Charles Dickens." Later, as we watched TV together, Tamar turned to David and raised her voice, snapping: "Turn down the volume. It's blowing my brains out!" Shortly after, her phone rang, and I overheard Tamar say, "Why are you breathing so loud right into the phone? It sounds like a hurricane!"

In the Middle East, and around the Mediterranean, often people talk loudly, interrupt, and exaggerate. They thrive on debate, negotiation, and confrontation. Imagine how many Arabic, Hebrew, Italian, Turkish, and Greek speakers might misinterpret the advice offered by Rumi, the 13th Century Persian poet:

> *"Raise your words, not your voice;*
> *It is rain that grows the flowers,*
> *Not thunder."*

Culture Through the Prism of Language

Many visitors to the U.S. are shocked by the amount of violence in our media, and the ease of purchasing guns. Some states allow guns in schools, places of worship, even bars. A few restaurants offer gun-carrying patrons special welcomes and discounts. In one Colorado restaurant, customers are greeted by a gun-toting waitress, according to a *Wall Street Journal* (August 4, 2014) article.

The many comments about guns I hear from foreigners have made me aware of how the culture of violence has influenced the way many Americans speak. Often unconsciously, we use the rhetoric and metaphors of guns in innocent interactions. I wrote about this in the piece below, entitled "Our Culture on the Firing Line."[1]

> With only 5% of the world's population, U.S. Americans now possess about 50% of the world's guns. Is it any wonder then that mass shootings in the U.S. have skyrocketed in the last decade? And in the wake of the grotesque massacre in Sandy Hook, gun sales have spiked dramatically. No wonder that sales of kids' bulletproof backpacks have soared, or that our culture more than ever is drenched in the language of guns!
>
> As I watch left and right-wing politicians and pundits "up in arms" on TV, battling in a "cross-fire" of blame, each side looking for a "smoking gun" to explain or cast blame for horrifying gun-related catastrophes, I've become increasingly aware of how our culture's preoccupations with guns are reflected even during innocent "shooting the breeze" conversations.

We often value the "straight shooter," yet we are wary of those who "shoot their mouths off," and those who "shoot from the hip," or glibly end an argument with a "parting shot." We caution colleagues to avoid "shooting themselves in the foot," and counsel them not to "shoot the messenger."

Without suspecting what drives our language, we are "blown away" by adorable photos of loved ones. At the movies, many audiences are thrilled by "shoot 'em up," "double-barreled action" scenes, or are excited by car chases where actors "gun" their engines.

I often ask friends to "shoot me" an email and I've encouraged job seekers to give an interview their "best shot" and "stick to their guns" during salary discussions. And if a job is offered, I might congratulate them for doing a "bang up" job.

In sensitive business negotiations, I've advised patience, urging clients to "trouble shoot" solutions, but to avoid "jumping the gun" and to be aware of "loaded" questions. To get the biggest "bang for the buck," I've recommended bringing the "big guns" to the table. We look for "silver bullet" solutions, hoping for "bulletproof" results. And when success is in sight, we say: "You're on target," or "you're going great guns!"

We encourage entrepreneurial risk taking, even if the project doesn't have a "shot in hell." Just "fire away" when you make that "killer" presentation, and if your idea is "shot down," don't be "gun shy." Just "bite the bullet" and go at it again, with "guns blazing." Don't be afraid to "shoot for the moon," even if it looks like a "shot in the dark."

Having worked as a university executive with students from more than 80 countries, I've noticed that the violent language in our songs and films strikes students from abroad, and they hear it bleeding into our political discourse. Many have asked me in amazement why it is even necessary to state that guns and ammunition are banned from university residence halls. Yet, "son of a gun," 26 colleges, in three states, allow guns on college campuses. And gun liberalization legislation for colleges is in the "cross hairs" in at least nine more states.

I've heard staff and students alike stressed by an approaching deadline, instinctively describing themselves as being "under the gun." Sometimes my colleagues have described emotional co-workers as "loose cannons" or having "hair trigger" personalities. And when a student has gone off "half-cocked," psychologists have advised employees to "keep their powder dry" and to review "bullet point" guidelines for handling volatile personalities.

In the same way that the U.S. is flooded with millions of guns (there are 90 guns per one hundred Americans), so, too, our newscasts—"sure as shootin'"—are exploding almost nightly with murder stories, reflecting the newsroom mantra: "If it bleeds, it leads."

When the local story becomes a national tragedy, there is "new ammunition" for both gun control supporters and opponents of banning firearms in such places as elementary schools, day care centers, churches, or even the neighborhood bar!

The world of guns has had our rhetoric in its sights for a very long time. And our wounded language—now more than ever with a gun to its head—is telling us that our culture is on the firing line.

The significance of violence, as well as sports, in U.S. American life is also reflected in boxing metaphors which, like gun metaphors, often are misunderstood by non-English speakers. In the early 20th century, boxing was a marquee American sport, along with baseball. Today, although it has lost some popularity, Americans unknowingly pepper their conversations with boxing metaphors. "Take off the gloves," and "stop pulling your punches," suggest it's time for serious confrontation. Other boxing expressions, such as calling someone a "heavyweight," a "lightweight," or a "knockout," can leave a foreigner puzzled, or as we might say, "on the ropes" or "down for the count." Becoming accustomed to a country and its language is what helps one to "roll with the punches" or even be "saved by the bell."

Basketball metaphors such as "full court press" and "slam dunk" frequently are heard in the competitive U.S. American business world. American football has grown considerably in popularity over the last several decades. People often talk about "end run" or "hail Mary" strategies, only to engage in "Monday morning quarterbacking" if the plans didn't succeed.

Baseball has historically been called the USA's "national pastime." Baseball metaphors are indelibly imprinted in American English, but often are confusing to visitors, especially in the boardroom. "Right off the bat" many foreign business people are "caught off base." If you're told that your presentation is "in the ball park," but hasn't "covered all the bases," is "the game over?" No, but next time, to avoid "striking out," you'd better "step up to the plate" and "keep your eyes on the ball." It's important to be prepared for both "hardball" and "softball" questions. This way, you're more likely to be a "big hit." Your American business partners even may say you've "pitched" a great idea with an attractive "ballpark figure." Clearly, it's a "new ball game" and your proposal may well be a success—a "home run."

***

"There is no such thing as a pretty good omelet."

"Better pay the baker than the doctor."
—French sayings

While living in Toulouse with a French family, I not only was struck by the exquisite food, but how conversations frequently focused on the food's aesthetic presentation: how well it was cooked, and how a particular herb might add to the taste, texture, or scent. The importance of food in French culture became more apparent as I noticed the extraordinary number of festivals devoted to a specific food: strawberries, melons, truffles, mushrooms, asparagus, olive oil, bread, soups, chestnuts, *foie gras*, crepes, even the celebrations of organ meat such as kidneys, liver, and lungs. Therefore, I wasn't surprised when, in 2010, UNESCO declared "lunch" in France to be among humanity's greatest cultural treasures.

The importance of food is reflected in the language, as well. Some of French President Francois Hollande's political opponents called him a "fragile strawberry," "a wobbly flan," "a marshmallow," or "*gauche caviar*" with the charisma of a "smelly sausage."

The expressions I collected in "Bicycling in the Yogurt: The French Food Fixation," illustrate how a culture's preoccupations shape the way language is used.[2]

> I was introduced to the pleasures of French cuisine, and its influence on the French language, as a university student hitchhiking through Normandy sampling butter, cream, and apple-brandy-suffused dishes.
>
> Struggling to express myself in village bistros, I realized the truth behind Mark Twain's observation that Intermediate French is not spoken in France. A friendly waiter, noting my frustration, reassured me saying, "*Je sais, c'est pas de la tarte,*" (I know, it's not pie), which means, "it's difficult." He went on to add, "*mais c'est pas la fin des haricots*" (but it's not the end of the string beans)—a strikingly French way of saying, "it's not the end of the world."
>
> A decade later, my French was much improved. While directing a U.S. American study abroad

program in Toulouse, my understanding of food's influence on the language deepened. Before taking a French cooking class with my 20 students, we stopped at an open-air market. Because the line to buy cheese was not moving, our impatient guide complained: "*on ne veut pas faire le poireau,*" (we don't want to be like a leek). Later, we learned the translation: to wait like a motionless leek in the ground. Now late for cooking class, our guide urged the van driver, "*appuyez sur le champignon!*" (press on the mushroom!)—meaning, "step on the gas!" Keeping a chef waiting simply would not do.

The students and I were struck by how carefully the chef conducted the lesson—artfully presenting and discussing the ingredients. The meal is serious business, not to be treated like a joke or, as the French say, "*c'était pas du flan ce cours de cuisine*" (like custard)! As we prepared a fruit salad, the chef mumbled "*oh purée!*" (mashed potatoes!), meaning "damn it!" and disdainfully discarded a blemished peach to preserve an aesthetically pleasing fruit plate.

During four years living in Strasbourg, Toulouse, and the island of Corsica, I learned how the French passion for eating and discussing food flavored the language in tasty and unusual ways, though some expressions are unique to different regions or generations. It began to make sense that endearing French metaphors are often rooted in the pleasures of taste. "What a nice person" is served up in French as *c'est une crème!* (it's cream), while *la crème de la crème* (the cream of creams), is the best of all. And "you are so energetic" takes on a carbohydrate-boost in French as *tu as la frite* (you have the French fry). To be in high spirits also can come from the fruit family, as in *tu as la pêche* (you have the peach), while *avoir la banane* (having a banana) is to have a big smile. And, of course, there's the affectionate *mon petit chou* (my little cabbage).

Allusions to food also season the language of love. A broken-hearted UC Berkeley student of mine from Marseille described her flirtatious boyfriend as *quelqu'un qui a un cœur d'artichaut* (Don Juan with the heart of an artichoke), offering each of his lovers a leaf from his heart. He was skilled at making romantic advances, or as my student put it, *faire du plat à quelqu'un* (serving up a dish), as a prelude to *aller aux fraises* (going off to the strawberries) to enjoy an erotic interlude.

Even insults and put-downs easily spring from the tongue as if from a farmers' market. An idiot or jerk, for example, can be described in French as *quel cornichon!* (what a pickle!), *une vraie courge* (an utter squash), *quelle nouille* (such a noodle), or *avoir un petit pois à la place du cerveau* (having a green pea in the brain). When struggling to drive in France, I've heard irate, gesturing French men speed past, yelling *"espèce d'andouille!"* (piece of sausage), roughly translated as "you imbecile!"

I remember a heated debate in a Paris café about a Gerard Depardieu film. A friend dismissed it as *un navet* (a turnip), a startling vegetable metaphor for a trashy film. When he called the actor a horrible drunk, an indignant Depardieu fan interrupted with: *"ferme ta boîte à Camembert!"* ("Shut your smelly Camembert mouth!")

Just as food evokes passion in France, its metaphorical expressions enliven debate. Interrupting a conversation is *ramener ta fraise* (to bring your strawberry). Being overly inquisitive about someone's private life could provoke an acerbic *"occupe-toi de tes oignons!"* (mind your own onions!), the French version of "mind your own business." But perhaps the classic French way of ending an argument is *"va te faire cuire un œuf,"* (go cook yourself an egg), or "go to hell."

Traveling through the Pyrénées with a French couple, my wife and I enjoyed great food and spirited conversations, especially about politics. When the husband praised Sarkozy, his wife sneered that the former President is overly dramatic: *"il fait tout un fromage de rien du tout"* (making a big cheese out of nothing). She added, *"on ne sait pas si c'est du lard ou du cochon"* (you can't tell if he's talking about pork fat or pork meat), that is, you can't tell if he's lying or telling the truth. And she believed Sarkozy had *des casseroles au cul* (casseroles hanging on his butt), or a scandalous past.

While serving as Dean of Students at an international college in Strasbourg, I was struck by how much my French colleagues valued using words precisely, reflected in the pervasive use of the verb *"préciser."* I chuckled when I heard some professors describe student papers that lacked clarity. They complained that these students were lost, *pédalant dans la choucroute* (bicycling in the sauerkraut). In other regions, one might say "bicycling in the yogurt" or "in the *couscous*." And then there's, *nageant dans le chocolat* (swimming in chocolate) and *patinant dans la mayonnaise* (skating in the mayonnaise)—getting nowhere. Outside the college, I heard other vivid ways of describing confusion such as *être dans le potage, être dans le pâté,* or *être dans les choux* (being in the soup, the *paté*, or the cabbages).

Recently, I saw an exasperated French TV commentator despair over the French economy by throwing up his hands exclaiming "*quelle salade!*" (what a salad!), or what a mess! And then he finished with "*les carottes sont cuites!*" (the carrots are cooked!) meaning, "it's all over."

If one is unemployed and grouchy, or as the French say, *pas dans son assiette* (not on your plate), landing a job would help to make things better or *mettre du beurre dans les épinards* (put butter on the spinach). Then it's time to *mettre la main a la pate* (put your hand in the dough), or get down to business. After all, you must *défendre ton bifteck* (defend your steak), as in "look out for your interests."

Speaking of steak, making a living is *gagner son bifteck* (to earn one's steak), while *faire son beurre* (to prepare one's butter), means making a profit. And *avoir de la galette* (to have a pancake) is to be rich. Assuming pancakes are your goal, you'll have to go all out, *mettre la sauce* (put on the sauce), and be prepared to make a strong sales pitch, *vendre ta salade* (selling your salad).

A UC Berkeley graduate student in computer science, from Tours, told me he was building a start-up company—*une jeune pousse* (a young sprout), and *ne pas savoir à quelle sauce on va être mangé* (didn't know what to expect or what sauce he would eat). He knew *avoir du pain sur la planche* (he had bread on the board), a lot of work to do, but realized that while dealing with potential investors he had to avoid *être roulé dans la farine* (being rolled in the flour), or duped. Otherwise, he risked *manger la grenouille* (eating the frog)—going bankrupt. He didn't want to end up *ne plus avoir un radis* (without a radish), or as we would say, without a cent, all his dreams for nothing—*pour des prunes*. Still, if he becomes successful like a Bill Gates, he's apt to be called *une grosse legume* (a large vegetable), and be among *le gratin* (the grated cheese), or the elite.

The versatility of the cheese metaphor in a country with hundreds of cheeses is not surprising. "A dessert without a cheese is like a beautiful woman with only one eye," observed Jean Brillat-Savarin in his *Physiology of Taste*. His famous 19th-century book exploring the nuances of cuisine is still sold in France. And no wonder, with a line like: "He who invents a new dish will have rendered humanity a greater service than the scientist who discovers a planet."

Today, as French supermarkets and fast food restaurants continue to proliferate, gourmands refuse to compromise or *couper la poire en deux* (cut the pear in two) in defending their culinary heritage. For more than twenty years, during *"La semaine du goût,"* (Taste Week), thousands of chefs visit schools across the country. They teach children to appreciate fine food; make a baguette and *mousse au chocolat*, appreciate a *bouillabaisse*, and learn the anatomy of the tongue. Restaurants with Michelin stars develop special meals for young children. And chefs are invited to daycare centers to prepare gourmet menus.

Will this unique early training insure the survival of the refined French palate and the nourishment of its language? A master chef is likely to respond, of course, *"mais oui, c'est du tout cuit"* (it's completely cooked)—it's in the bag.

My colleague, Dianne Hofner Saphiere, spent years working the interface between Japanese and Western cultures. She is fascinated with how Japanese use onomatopoeia (擬音語 or *Giongo*) to describe many things, including food and its taste, texture, and temperature. While working in Japan, Dianne heard some Westerners comment that these words sound like children's "gibberish." Yet, in Dianne's opinion, Giongo are vital to the Japanese language and rich with deep connotations. In her blog post, "Want to Feel Ukiuki, Pichipichi and Pinpin? Japanese Food Onomatopoeia," she shows how the simple sounds of these onomatopoeia words carry heavily nuanced meanings.[3]

I have been quite *ujiuji* (melancholy, ウジウジ) in recent weeks, feeling *uzu-uzu* (a burning desire, ウ

ズウズ) to hear and speak Japanese. Living in a small city in Mexico, *zenzen* (almost never, 全然) can('t) I hear Japanese, and my heart gets *shoboshobo* (sad, ショボショボ).

Joe's recent blog post on the French food fixation only fueled more *tsukuzuku* (heartfelt thinking, ツクズク) on my part. As you may have already figured out from my *wazawaza* (purposeful, ワザワザ) language, I've been thinking about Japanese sound symbolism, particularly in the context of food.

Whether you eat *gatsugatsu* (gobble or devour, ガツガツ) or *potsupotsu* (little by little, ポツポツ), if you want to talk about food in Japanese you will be using words that mimetically represent feelings and senses. As the originators of the concept of *umami* (pleasant savory taste—one of the five basic tastes), Japanese tend to *mokumoku* (munch, モクモク) the way they listen: with all their senses. Taste, texture, and temperature, sound, smell and sensation...all are important elements that combine to keep people *ukiuki* (cheerful, ウキウキ), *pichipichi* (young and vigorous, ピチピチ), and *pinpin* (in good health, ピンピン).

While many people think of Japanese food as the tastes and textures of sashimi or sushi, a typical meal may also contain *iroriro-na* (a variety of, いろいろ) food including boiled, broiled, fried or pickled dishes, a soup and *hokahoka* (warm, ホカホカ) steamed white rice. Is your stomach starting to *guuguu* (growl hungrily, グウグウ)?

For the fresh or raw component of your meal, would you like something *shakishaki* (シャキシャキ)—crisp as in veggies or fruits, e.g., lettuce washed in cold water? Or would you prefer something more *korikori* (コリコリ)—crunchy and crisp, as in fresh raw abalone? Be sure to rinse the abalone well, so it doesn't taste *jarijari* (gritty, ジャリジャリ) or *zarazara* (coarse, ザラザラ). Maybe you want something *sharishari* シャリシャリ—tangy and juicy, like an Asian *nashi* pear or sherbet? Or is your tongue like mine, and craves the *piripiri* (sting, ピリピリ) of *wasabi* or *fugu* (blowfish)? Any of these dishes will require *chokichoki* (cutting with a knife, チョキチョキ) preparation.

A boiled dish in our meal might include pumpkin *nimono*, stewed *hokuhoku* (steamy and dense but not soggy, ホクホク), or something more *furufuru* (soft and jiggly, フルフル) like boiled eggs. Maybe we should make some *chikuwa* (fish paste roll) for *oden* till it's *buyobuyo* (swollen and soft, ブヨブヨ) and *fuwafuwa* (fluffy, フワフワ)? Oh, that sounds good! There are just so many possibilities! So many tastes and textures!

There are *madamada* (still, まだまだ) *ippai-ippai* (lots, いっぱい•いっぱい) more onomatopoeia to consider. What about a main dish? Shall we eat something *sakusaku* (freshly cooked crisp and light, サクサク) like tempura shrimp? I could fry it till the shrimp inside are *puripuri* (crispy with a nice resistance, プリプリ) and the breading is *poripori* (quietly crunchy, ポリポリ). Perhaps you are really craving the *shikoshiko* (chewy, elastic firmness, シコシコ) of some *udon* noodles? Never over-boil the pasta so it becomes *betobeto* (sticky and gummy, ベトベト); rather, you'll probably be *wakuwaku* (trembling with excitement, ワクワク) to eat your *tsurutsuru* (shiny and slurpy, ツルツル) noodles and *gabugabu* (drink heartily, ガブガブ) a beer!

Instead of your normal bowl of rice you might enjoy something a bit more *mochimochi* (soft, sticky and chewy, モチモチ) or *netoneto* (glutinous and gummy, ネトネト) like sticky rice. Maybe rice that's a bit more *pasapasa* (dry, パサパサ), like jasmine rice, sounds appetizing? The *kunkun* (smell, クンクン) is so nice! *Tabitabi* (once in a while, 度々), though, I like the *parapara* (moist but loose, パラパラ) of fried rice.

Even though by now you are *panpan* (full, パンパン), *pukupuku* (swollen, プクプク), and maybe even *kokkurikokkuri* (nodding off, コックリ • コックリ), a *karikari* (hard and crispy, カリカリ) biscotti, a *fukafuka* (soft and fluffy, フカフカ) cream puff, or even some *purupuru* (wiggly, jiggly, プルプル) *kanten* (gelatin) for dessert might refresh your soul. Maybe just a handful of something *punyupunyu* (プニュプニュ), like some gummies?

After such a big meal your throat may feel *karakara* (thirsty, カラカラ). I'd definitely recommend a *chibichibi* (sip, チビチビ) of a *kachikachi* (ice cold,

カチカチ), *shuwashuwa* (sparkling, シュワシュワ) beverage over a *betabeta* (sticky, ベタベタ) dessert wine. It can help settle any *mukamuka* (queasiness, ムカムカ) you might have.

What if you're not really that hungry, and you just want to *mushamusha* (munch, ムシャムシャ)? You might want the *paripari* (thin and crispy, パリパリ) of *nori* (toasted seaweed) or chips. Sometimes, though, we crave a louder *pachipachi* (crispy snapping sound, パチパチ), like the *baribari* (loud crunchiness, バリバリ) of *sembei* (rice crackers) or the *kachikachi* (crisp firmness, カチカチ) of *arare* (another kind of rice cracker).

***

"Eating is Heaven."
—Ancient Chinese proverb

"Our lives are not in the laps of the gods, but in the laps of our cooks."
—Lin Yutang

After telling a Chinese friend about the variety of French food metaphors, and Dianne's Japanese onomatopoeia expressions, he gave me *Food in Chinese Culture*, published by the Ministry of Culture of the People's Republic of China. It inspired me to write "The Squid Has Been Fried."[4,5]

Long suspecting that Chinese, like French, reflects a heightened preoccupation with food, I immediately turned to the chapter, "Food as Metaphor." I learned that China's classics contain many examples of food metaphors illustrating political, social, and philosophical principles. The philosopher Laozi, for instance, observed that, "one should govern a large country as one would cook a small fish—very gently" (治大國若烹小鮮; 治大国若烹小鲜).

Yanzi, another famous Chinese philosopher, noted that "harmonious government, like cooking a fish, requires a proper blend of policy, just as cooking a fish requires the proper blend of vinegar, soy sauce, salt, and plum." (和如羹 焉，水火醯醢鹽梅，以烹魚肉，燀之以薪，宰夫和之，齊之 以味，濟其不及，以洩其過; 和如羹焉，水火醯醢盐梅，以 烹鱼肉，燀之以薪，宰夫和之，齐之以味，济其不及，以洩 其过) If ministers were to follow their ruler's behavior blindly, it would be like boiling a fish in plain water; who would want to eat it?

Hearing this, a Chinese friend reminded me that fish frequently are associated with prosperity in Chinese culture, though "climbing up a tree in search of fish" (緣木求魚; 缘木求鱼) is to do the impossible.

Chinese philosophers, according to *Food in Chinese Culture*, also used food imagery to explain literary creation. "It was said that a writer's ideas are like grains of uncooked rice. When the grains are boiled into porridge, that is prose; when they are fermented into wine, that is poetry." (生活的 素材是米，散文是米飯，詩歌是酒; 生活的素材是米，散 文 是米饭，诗歌是酒)

In business, "being handed a rice bowl" (給飯碗; 给饭碗) is to be hired, while "having your rice bowl broken" (砸飯碗; 砸饭碗) is to be fired. A Shanghai-born MBA student explained that if you protest being fired, the boss' response might be: "the rice is cooked" (生米煮成熟飯; 生米煮成熟饭), meaning it's too late to do anything about it (my decision is final). Perhaps you should have just performed your duties, as "talk does not cook rice" (光說不練; 光说不练). Still, a Chinese employee might counter with, "I won't bow for five measures of rice" (我不為五斗米折腰 我不为五斗米折腰), suggesting he refuses to do anything demeaning for money. Bottom line: "the squid had been fried" (炒魷魚; 炒鱿鱼)—he was fired. Because the fried squid is shriveled, there is a serious loss of face.

Some of my other Chinese-speaking students remind me that in business and other activities, one should remember that "if you pick up a sesame seed, you may drop a watermelon" (丟了西瓜撿芝麻（撿了芝麻丟了西瓜）;丢了西瓜捡芝麻 (捡了芝麻丢了西瓜), or lose sight of important issues because you focus on trivial matters. And certainly one should avoid "stale grain and uncooked sesame" (陳穀子爛芝麻; 陈谷子烂芝麻)—boring, unimportant gossip.

According to Gong Wenxiang, author of *Food in Chinese Culture*, the Chinese word *shi* means "to eat," as well as "to earn a living." So perhaps it's not surprising that "to eat land" (靠地（田產）吃飯; 靠地（田产）吃饭) means to get income by renting out farm land, while "to eat salary" (靠薪 水吃飯; 靠 薪水吃饭) means to work for wages, and "to eat strength" (靠勞力吃飯; 靠劳力吃饭) means to survive via physical labor.

A Mandarin-speaking foodie friend described other "eating" expressions that reflect consuming, digesting, or absorbing. "Stuffing a duck" (填鴨; 填鸭), to prepare a fine meal, also can refer to studying hard, or cramming to ensure excellent test results. Losing a competition causes people to "eat vinegar" (吃醋), and beating mahjong or chess opponents is often expressed as "eating their pieces" (吃牌), with the loser expected "to eat bitter" (吃苦)—to be able to withstand difficulty. Perhaps this is why the plum blossom is a national Chinese symbol; flowering in winter, it overcomes cold, just as the Chinese people survive and thrive despite hardship.

I suspect that the examples here are but a bland reflection of the rich banquet of Chinese eating and food metaphors that are yet to be savored by non-Chinese speakers. After all, according to a Chinese proverb "eating is even more important than the emperor." (吃飯皇帝大; 吃饭皇帝大)

A Stranger in a Strange Land

While language reveals, from my point of view, a certain level of preoccupation with food in French, Japanese, and Chinese cultures, eating across cultures can reveal striking cultural contrasts. Here's how Muhammed Ali Shahidy, a women's rights activist from Afghanistan, while studying psychology at Norwich University, describes the culture shock of his first meal in the United States.[6]

> I never imagined that ordering lunch in the USA would be an ordeal for me. Back in Afghanistan, I taught English for several years. I watched countless Hollywood movies, and worked with foreigners for almost four years. I performed well on standardized tests of English, or at least in English, like the TOEFL exam and the SAT. So I never expected that bread, cheese, or a drink would challenge my English abilities.

> The day I arrived in the U.S., my plane was diverted to Raleigh-Durham International Airport in North Carolina. While waiting for my next flight, I went to one of the cafeterias close to my gate. People were lined up, so I went to the end of the line. It was crowded, and the staff was working hurriedly. Since I had no idea what cuisines they served, I decided to order just a sandwich. I thought that's the simplest, easiest, and fastest food to get. It was my turn to place my order. I asked the lady for a chicken sandwich. She asked, "What do you want it on?" I stared at her quizzically and was speechless for a moment.

> The lady asked, more loudly this time, "What bun do you want?" I said, "Just a chicken sandwich, please." The lady replied impatiently, "Yes, I know. But what bun?"

I didn't know what to say. I couldn't understand her. Then I thought maybe she was asking about the sauce. "Hmm... it doesn't matter," I responded. She seemed irritated, and then asked rapidly, "Cheddar, Pepperjack, Swiss, Provolone, or American?" This is what I heard, "chedie, paper jack, Swiss (the country), Provolo, or American (also, the country)?" I wondered, "Are they different types of chicken? Does chicken differ from one country to another?" I stared at her mutely as my brain tried to decipher the meaning of those words.

Starting to sweat, I acted as if I didn't understand English at all. Then I said, "American, please!" maybe because that was the last option and the easiest to remember. Then she asked, "fountain drink or bottled soda?"

You know what? I just wanted to cancel my order and stay hungry instead of standing in front of this hasty female waitress who seemed frustrated by me, and whose offers I couldn't understand at all. My anxiety mounted in this crowded line of hungry customers who were all waiting for me to finish my order, and I ... I just didn't know what to say. I said, "I just want a soft drink. That's it ma'am." She said, "I know, but bottled or fountain?" That was a lot of pressure—more pressure than the TOEFL exam. I never imagined that buying a sandwich in the U.S. would be this challenging and cause me so much embarrassment. The hundred-dollar bill in my hand was damp with my sweat, squeezed and crumpled. "Bottled, please!" although I had no idea what the difference was.

When I paid for my food, I stood in my place, expecting my food to be delivered to the counter instantly. The lady said, "Sir, this is your slip. Please take a seat and we will call you when your food is ready." I nodded like a parrot that understands everything people tell him, and walked away. But now I wondered how she would call me. While sitting at my table, I watched and listened vigilantly. I realized she was calling customers by number. I stared at the number on my slip and listened intently. When I heard my number, I took my food and found a seat far away from the cafeteria.

As I ate my first meal in the U.S., I pondered over the fact that I knew words like "abrogate," "conflagration," and "inexorable," but not the words "bun" or "fountain drink." I could comfortably write professional technical proposals and review solicitations in English but broke into a sweat ordering a chicken sandwich. And then I realized, my lunch ordeal wasn't an English deficiency at all, but rather a cultural difference. I had just arrived from a country with very few options—bread is bread, and cheese is cheese. And if we're lucky enough to have any choices, it's usually the choice of yes or no.

When Muhammed Ali Shahidy tried ordering that chicken sandwich, he felt like a stranger in a strange land.

Yet, understanding a new culture and its language is more than crossing national, regional, ethnic, religious, or economic borders. It also entails understanding the cultures of our parents and children...and cultural disconnects between generations, as Margaret Mead observed:

> *"A typical elder's remark: 'You know, I have been young, and you have never been old.'*
> *A typical young person's response: 'You have never been young in the world I am young in.'"*

In 1985, an 80-year-old author friend in Manhattan complained about the difficulties finding a typewriter ribbon. "Why not try a computer?" I asked. "It will make your editing easier." "That's an insurmountable monumental hurdle," she said with a sigh. "I'm beginning to feel like a fossil in my own time."

I did, too, after sending out an email to thirty of my former UC students, offering a complimentary international career coaching class. When I spotted a student on campus, I asked why no one had responded to my invitation. "TLTR," she said. Puzzled, I asked what it means. The response: "Too long to read." For students living in the faster, abbreviated world of texting and Twitter, lengthy emails like mine are becoming obsolete. In-depth conversations and listening to voice mail messages are increasingly rare, or, as some put it: "TLTL"—too long to listen.

While presenting a cross-cultural communication workshop for a group of Google employees, I asked participants to take out pens and paper, and they looked surprised. I'd forgotten that to young techies, writing on paper seems almost as prehistoric as chiseling on a stone table. We were at Google, of all places!

***

*"Getting information on the Internet is like
taking a drink from a fire hydrant."*
—Mitchell Kapor

Overwhelmed by the information explosion and endless possibilities of Google searches, many of us have less time for face-to-face interaction, which increases chances for misunderstanding. Many friends, especially those over the age of forty, complain that messages from younger people seem terse and impersonal. In text messages, greetings like "dear," and polite phrases like "How are you?" or "May I help you?" are rare, replaced by formulaic acronyms. "Thank you" has become "TU;" "You're welcome" is now "YW"; "PLZ" means "Please"; and a cryptic "RUOK?" is "How are you?" Recently, I was puzzled by "HTH"; translation—"Happy to help."

When I was at Twitter headquarters in San Francisco, a twenty-something employee told me, "We're polite, but we just express things differently." She went on to describe that her parents, accustomed to judging the quality of a conversation by tone of voice, facial expressions, and gestures, complain that her Tweets and texts are impersonal and rushed.

Even some employees of Twitter and Facebook find communicating with their younger siblings perplexing. For example, "ATM" means "automated teller machine" to many of us, but to a teen, it currently means "at the moment." "HK" can mean "Hong Kong," but to a 13-year-old it signifies "Hugs and kisses." Her "LOL" text to her mother was lost in translation. The 50-year-old mother thought it meant what she wanted to hear, "Lots of love," but her daughter meant, "Laugh out loud." Her father and older brothers were stumped by "OFOTD," but her girlfriends understood her gender-specific message. Translation: "Outfit of the day."

While parents struggle to understand the language of texts and tweets, their children are using letter codes to hide secrets. For example, to alert friends about prying parents, a teen may text "POS" ("Parents over shoulder"), "MPRC," which means, "My parents are coming," or "P911" ("Parent alert"). And "KPC"? It means "Keep parents clueless." Sometimes, when teens feel rapid-fire acronyms are limiting communication, they may request "F2F" ("Face-to-face") time, or they may thumb-type, "LMIRL" (Let's meet in real life).

***

"A rumor goes in one ear and out of many mouths."
—Chinese proverb

"If everybody thought before they spoke,
the silence would be deafening."
—George Barzan

Texts and tweets are outlets for fast information. According to *Business Week*, when Hurricane Sandy slammed New York in October 2012, CNN staffers read Tweets that the New York Stock Exchange was inundated with three feet of water. They ran the Tweets as news. Social media went viral with eye-popping photos of scuba divers in the New York subway. All the reports were false.

After the earthquake and tsunami hit Japan, Tweets claiming to be from CNN and BBC were sent. The fake Tweets announced that Japan's nuclear reactors were going to melt down, killing eighty percent of the Japanese population and half of the people on the West Coast of the U.S. and Canada. The instantaneous delivery of lies had the potential to cause mass hysteria. The lightning speed of social media permits the spread of information, with no time to verify its veracity. As Mark Twain is said to have observed: "A lie can travel half way around the world while the truth is putting on its shoes."

Iran's semi-official Fars News Agency published a major story in 2012 with this lead: "According to the results of a Gallup poll released Monday, the overwhelming majority of rural white Americans said they would rather vote for Iranian president Mohamed Ahmadinejad than U.S. President Obama." The Iranian news story included a quote, from a resident of West Virginia, who said that Ahmadinejad "takes national defense seriously and, unlike Obama, he'd never let some gay protesters tell him how to run his country." The Fars report went on to refer to a Gallup poll indicating that sixty percent of rural whites said they respected Ahmadinejad for not trying to hide the fact that he's Muslim.

What Fars didn't understand was that the source for its article, *The Onion*, is a satirical publication that presents the absurd as real news.[7]

Because digital communication does not easily convey irony and sarcasm within—and especially across—cultures, the chances of misunderstanding are increased. When irony is lost in translation, fiction easily can be perceived as fact.

Questions and Activities, Chapter Four

1. What one intends to say is not always what is heard, as in the "My calendar is packed" story at the beginning of this chapter. Think of some examples within your own culture and language, when what you meant to communicate was misinterpreted or heard differently by the person who received your message. What are some possible explanations for the miscommunications?

   Can you think of an occasion when your words, when literally translated into another language, may have meant something entirely different from what you intended to communicate? What did the message mean to the receiver? Does the message received suggest something about the values that might be associated with your words in the receiver's language and culture that are different from your own?

2. Log on to your *Culture Detective Online* subscription and click on the *Indonesia* Package. Go to the Incidents tab and click on "How Many Mothers." Review the incident and consider how you would summarize Words and Actions as objectively as possible; fill in that portion of the Worksheet. Compare the behavior of the Indonesian Manager and the French Expatriate. Next, think about how you would explain the conflict between the Indonesian Manager and the French Expatriate. What are the Values, Beliefs and Personal Common Sense of each? Fill in that portion of the Worksheet. Then, compare the values and beliefs of the Indonesian Manager with the French Expatriate. Now, understanding that the conflict was driven by a different interpretation of the word "mother," how would you

propose to bridge their differences in a way that would honor their contrasting concepts or values? Fill in the Bridges portion of the Worksheet. Compare your ideas in the Building Bridges section with those of the Authors.

3. What definitions and associations do you have with the following words: friendship, family, politeness, privacy, compromise, deadline, freedom, individualism, happiness, beautiful, teacher, equality? Think of examples that illustrate the meaning of these words for you. Discuss with friends, colleagues or classmates from other cultures the definitions and associations they have with all or some of these words. Where their definitions or associations may differ from yours, what might this suggest about personal and/or cultural differences?

4. How language is used is often a source of confusion across cultures. What do the following styles of communication mean to you: A loud vs. a soft voice when trying to convince someone of your ideas; turn-taking vs. interrupting in casual conversations; exaggeration vs. understatement when offering an opinion; use of long periods of silence vs. rapid responses to a question; expressing emotions freely vs. keeping emotions hidden with strangers; stating disagreements directly vs. expressing them indirectly. Compare and contrast your responses with groups of individuals from three or more cultures. What does each style of communicating mean to the various individuals from these cultures?

For a perspective on a variety of communication styles in another culture, click on the *Singapore* Package in your *Cultural Detective Online* subscription. Go to the Supplementary Materials tab and click on "Singaporean Communication Styles." Discuss with friends, colleagues or classmates how your respective styles of communication compare and contrast with those described in the Singapore overview. What are some of the contrasting values that help explain the differing communication styles described?

If you wish, click on the Incidents tab, then on "Create your own Incident," and follow the instructions to write a story from your own experience of miscommunication involving language or communication style differences. Analyze that story using the *Cultural Detective Worksheet* and ask a friend or colleague to join you.

Notes

1. Joe Lurie, "Culture on the Firing Line," *Cultural Detective Blog*, January 22, 2013:
http://blog.culturaldetective.com/2013/01/22/our-culture-on-the-firing-line/

2. Joe Lurie, "Bicycling in the Yogurt: the French Food Fixation," *Cultural Detective Blog*, May 29, 2012:
http://blog.culturaldetective.com/2012/05/29/bicycling-in-the-yogurt-the-french-food-fixation/

3. Dianne Hofner Saphiere, "Want to Feel Ukiuki, Pichipichi and Pinpin? Japanese Food Onomatopoeia," *Cultural*

Detective Blog, June 19, 2012:
http://blog.culturaldetective.com/2012/06/19/want-to-feel-ukiuki-pichipichi-and-pinpin-japanese-food-onomatopoeia/

4. Joe Lurie, "The Squid Has Been Fried," *Cultural Detective Blog*, June 28, 2012:
http://blog.culturaldetective.com/2012/06/28/the-squid-has-been-fried-language-culture-and-the-chinese-food-fixation/

5. Chia-Ying Sophia Pan, from Columbia University, wrote the script versions of the key Chinese expressions. The first set of characters is traditional Chinese as written in Taiwan and Hong Kong; the second set is simplified Chinese as written in the PRC. One set of characters means both versions are identical.

6. Muhammed Ali Shahidy gave us permission to republish "Culture Shock: My First Meal," which originally appeared in *The Chameleon*, Norwich University's literary journal, in April 2014.

7. "Iranian News Agency Plagiarizes the Onion," *The New York Times*, Sept. 28, 2012 and CNN report, Sept. 29, 2012.

CHAPTER FIVE

Minefields and Mind-Openers in the News

"The earth is a beehive; we enter by the same door but live in different cells."
—African proverb

As the global marketplace grows, sometimes product names are mistranslated in astonishing ways. IKEA, the Swedish multinational company that sells in over forty countries, uses Swedish names for about 9,000 of its branded products. One product, IKEA's *Jatterbra* plant pot, didn't sell well in Thailand. Why? Because in Thai, the word *Jatterbra* sounds like a crude term for sex. To avoid committing more translation *faux pas*, IKEA hired Thai linguists.[1] IKEA also changed the name of its workbench when it discovered why its English-speaking customers found the name *Fartfull* so humorous.

***

"Translation is the art of failure."
—Umberto Eco

When marketing across cultures, and even within countries, companies must be sensitive to language. An appealing name in one language might be offensive in another. A British company spent millions of dollars launching its new curry sauce, *Bundh*, but the negative response among curry-loving Punjabi speakers was surprising: in Punjabi, *bundh* means "ass." When Microsoft was promoting its search engine "Bing" in China, it discovered that in Mandarin Chinese, Bing sounds like "illness," and it also can mean "pancake" depending on which tone (3rd or 4th) is used. Microsoft changed the name to the more commercially appealing *biying*—which means, "seek and you shall find."[2]

Changing a brand or an established company name can be costly, complex, and embarrassing. When Buick was promoting its Lacrosse cars in Canada, teenagers in French-speaking Quebec snickered. They use the titillating word *lacrosse* when talking about masturbation.[3] Toyota's Fiera model sparked a controversy in Puerto Rico, where *fiera* means "ugly woman." And why did Ford's Pinto model flop in Brazil? In Brazilian Portuguese slang, *pinto* means "small penis."[4] Branding experts say being culturally blind to multiple meanings of a name can scar a company's reputation. Honda found it exasperating to sell its *Fitta* car in Sweden. The translation is naughty, apt for a porn star; in Swedish, *fitta* means female genitalia.[5]

Japan's second-largest tourist agency, Kinki Nippon Tourism, is named after the Kinki region in western Japan. When English-speakers began requesting unusual sex tours, the company changed its name from *Kinki* (pronounced kinky) to KNT Tourism.[6] And in May 2014, Japan's Kinki University announced it would change its name to Kindai University, to stop laughter, and to attract more English-speaking exchange students to its new international studies faculty.

In 1923, the Italo Suisse Chocolate Company was founded. In 1996, to boost sales, it sweetened its name to "Instant Seduction, Instant Satisfaction"—ISIS. In 2014, with the violent rise of ISIS (The Islamic State of Iraq and Syria) the chocolate company changed its name to "*Liebeert*" after the company's Belgian owners.[7] In September 2014, a tech start-up (a joint-venture involving AT&T, T-Mobile, and Verizon Wireless) changed the name of its payment app from "Isis Wallet" to "Softcard" to avoid the comparison with the notorious terrorist organization. In California, the $4.3 billion biotech firm, Isis Pharmaceuticals, Inc., has used the name for more than 25 years. Its CEO, Stanley Crooke, says he's not changing their name, but that the terrorist group is welcome to change theirs.

According to the U.S. Patent and Trademark Office, more than 270 products, services, and businesses have trademarks with the name Isis. Businesses aren't required to register their names, so no one knows how many more companies use Isis, which is also the name of an Egyptian goddess.

Getting lost in translation can cause serious problems for global businesses and have unintended consequences in the world of diplomacy. Akbar Zeb, former Director General of Pakistan's Foreign Ministry, served in the U.S., Canada, India, and South Africa. His family name, Zeb, means "someone with good countenance." But when the respected diplomat was selected to become Pakistan's Ambassador to Saudi Arabia, he didn't serve. Why? In Arabic, the name "Akbar Zeb" means "the biggest penis"[8]— an unacceptable public face for an ambassador to Saudi Arabia.

What Did That Apology Really Mean?

Just as many words aren't easily translated across languages, concepts can be misunderstood across cultures. For example, how is "apology" understood by different cultures? When the *USS Greeneville*, a U.S. Navy nuclear-powered attack submarine, surfaced off Oahu, Hawaii, it accidentally hit a Japanese fishing ship, the *Ehime Maru*. Nine Japanese, including four high school trainee students, were killed.

Two days later, on February 22, 2001, U.S. President George W. Bush gave this apology on TV: "I want to reiterate what I said to the Prime Minister of Japan: I'm deeply sorry about the accident that took place; our nation is sorry." U.S. Secretary of State Colin Powell and Secretary of Defense Donald Rumsfeld also publicly apologized. The U.S. Ambassador to Japan, Tom Foley, personally apologized to both the Emperor of Japan and to Prime Minister Mori.[9]

Several years later, the Japan-America Student Conference held at the Japanese Cultural Center of Hawaii reviewed the incident and discussed differing cultural perceptions of the meaning of "apology."[10] For the Japanese, an apology from the American ship's Commander came late, and it was crucial to convey his personal empathy. Even though President Bush and other officials had expressed official apologies, the Japanese felt that the Commander needed to apologize directly to the families, in public, as an expression of his personal awareness of their grief. At the same time, one Japanese family member even asked that the Commander kneel and bow his head in front of the families—the highest form of Japanese apology. In Japan, apology is a ritual, generally without the legal implications as might be interpreted in the U.S.

From the U.S. American perspective, an apology, in a case like this, might imply guilt and legal responsibility. The Commander's delay in apologizing could be explained in terms of an ongoing legal investigation, which might result in compensation damages. At that time, the American expression of "sincere regret" simply was insufficient to communicate empathy to the Japanese. And the Japanese couldn't comprehend the U.S. legal constraints. While the two conflicting notions of apology were the source of ongoing diplomatic tensions, the U.S. Commander eventually apologized to the ship's survivors and victims' families.

Sometimes, there are serious diplomatic issues due to cultural misunderstandings of differing "rules" of interpersonal and state-to-state apologies. When a U.S. surveillance plane collided with a Chinese military jet off China's southern coast in 2001, there was another clash of perspectives relating to the concept of apology.[11] From the U.S. perspective, the aggressive Chinese pilot was at fault, and caused the U.S. plane to make an emergency landing, without permission, at a Chinese military base on Hainan Island. The Chinese pilot's plane crashed, and he died at sea.

The issue caused several cross-cultural complications. While the U.S. government felt it had the right to make "deterrence" surveillance flights over international waters, for hundreds of years the Chinese have considered the area their territory. When translated into Chinese, the English word "deterrence" carries a connotation that means "threats" and "bullying."

Most importantly, the Chinese considered its pilot's death an affront to their collective national dignity. For China to regain lost face, a public American apology was necessary. From the U.S. American government's perspective, the aggressive Chinese pilot caused the incident, so an apology would indicate that the U.S. was guilty.

Americans were being held on the Hainan Island military base; to secure their release, the U.S. government expressed "regret" for the Chinese pilot's death. For Chinese-speakers, the word "regret" is unacceptable, because it doesn't acknowledge "guilt." Secretary of State Colin Powell performed a delicate diplomatic dance and said the U.S. was "sorry" for the loss of the Chinese pilot. For the U.S., the word "sorry" didn't acknowledge guilt, but it did permit the Chinese to translate "sorry" in a way that acknowledged guilt.

Another clash of U.S. and Chinese values arose when newly appointed U.S. Ambassador Gary Locke, who is Chinese-American, first arrived at Beijing Airport with his family. No large American entourage accompanied them. They traveled via commercial jet, carried their own luggage, and departed in an ordinary car, not a limousine.

Many Chinese were astonished to see photos of the U.S. Ambassador buying his own coffee, which, from his point of view, could be seen as demonstration of the U.S. American value of equality and informality. On Chinese social media, many ordinary people admired his down-to-earth behavior, which was a stark contrast to the formal power displays of many Chinese officials.

However, Chinese state-run media often took a different view. It described the Ambassador's unceremonious style as unsuitable for a diplomat representing the U.S., and as disrespectful and embarrassing to Chinese leaders.[12] One influential Chinese government newspaper even accused the U.S. of using its Ambassador to incite political chaos in China.

Six months before the November 2014 Asia-Pacific Economic Cooperation summit opened in Beijing, the Chinese Communist Party launched a campaign to teach Beijingers some Western forms of etiquette, such as not spitting on the street and staying in line. After all, China was hosting 21 world leaders. But several times during the ceremonies in Beijing, cameras caught President Obama chewing gum. Chinese media, accustomed to the formal stiff Chinese party leadership style, "chewed out" President Obama. Many critics took to *Sina Weibo*, the Chinese version of Twitter: "This is the American manner, but in traditional Chinese culture, it is immature and not serious behavior!" Yin Hong, a professor of journalism at Beijing's Tsinghua University, posted this: "We made this meeting so luxurious, with singing and dancing, but see Obama, stepping out of his car chewing gum like an idler." Another user labeled Obama a "rapper."

In other Asian countries, chewing gum also is often considered a social faux pas. Singapore bans importing gum; in Japan, chewing gum is a no-no, especially while conducting business.

When President Obama met Queen Elizabeth, one Twitter user grumbled: "And #Obama welcomed the Queen with chewing gum in his mouth...#shocking #boor." President Obama even chewed away at his own Inauguration in 2013. When he was viewing the 2015 India Republic Day Parade in New Delhi with Prime Minister Modi, he was chewing gum.

What brand of gum does President Obama favor, you ask? Nicorette®. The White House physician recommended President Obama chew nicotine gum to help combat his smoking habit. What brands of gum do the Chinese chew?

Wrigley® is the most popular. The U.S. American company controls about half the gum market in China. And it's growing: the Chinese chew a whopping 14 billion sticks of gum annually, the Asia Times reported.[13] But chewing gum at formal state functions is unacceptable.

The importance of showing appropriate respect for power in autocratic or Confucian-influenced societies was illustrated when Microsoft founder Bill Gates casually greeted South Korea's President, Park Geun-hye, in 2013. Wearing an unbuttoned jacket, Gates kept his left hand in his pants pocket. His informal greeting was widely interpreted in Korea as rude and disrespectful. It was such an affront to Korean national pride that the story and photos made front-page news throughout South Korea.

This was not the first time the laid-back billionaire had met heads of state. When Gates greeted former South Korean President Lee Myung-bak, and French Presidents Francois Hollande and Nicolas Sarkozy, he also kept one hand in his pants pocket.[14]

While Gates might profit from some cultural sensitivity training, a number of South Koreans think their media's criticism of Gates was one-dimensional. As one Korean tweeted: "Please people, don't think your Confucian mindset is a universal norm in other parts of the world."[15]

A few years ago, a diplomatic crisis arose between Norway and India due to an apparent clash of cultural values. An Indian couple, living in Norway, were accused of abusing their three-year-old son and one-year-old daughter. Norway's Protective Child Services placed the two children in foster care because the children slept in their parents' bed, the parents had no diaper-changing table, and they fed their children with their hands (a form of force-feeding, according to some Norwegians).

The Indian press and its diplomats attacked the Norwegians for cultural insensitivity and racism. Eating with the hands, sleeping with one's parents, and changing diapers without a table are normal behavior in India and in many other countries.

Because Norway's Child Protective Services would not comment publically, citing reasons of confidentiality, the story began feeding two different narratives: one in the Norwegian media and one in the Indian media; one portraying child abuse, the other suggesting cultural insensitivity. Later, it was revealed that the Indian father had become estranged from his wife, claiming she had a serious psychological problem, and had assaulted him many times. In retrospect, domestic violence became a possible explanation for removing the children from their parents' home.[16]

Indian and Norwegian diplomats finally agreed to return the children to India, in the care of their uncle, the father's brother. But in January a Calcutta high court ruled that the children belonged to the mother.[17]

Whatever misunderstandings some Indians and Norwegians may have about each other's cultures, one thing is clear, as John Lennon said, "The more I see, the less I know for sure."

Cultural Misperceptions and Violence

A few Afghani soldiers, serving with U.S. Americans and other NATO troops, killed more than 50 Western soldiers in 2012. Reasons provided for these "insider" killings ranged from Afghani soldiers using forged records to hide their Taliban ties, to their taking orders from opium drug lords. Some coalition officials also blamed lack of cultural knowledge for creating an atmosphere of distrust between Afghan and coalition troops.[18]

The rising number of killings by Afghanis serving with NATO troops deepened mistrust so much that the Afghan military produced an 18-page brochure, in the *Dari* language, to educate its troops about cultural misunderstandings of their Western counterparts. "In the area of cultural awareness, we are trying to educate our soldiers to understand the sensitivities of the culture of the Western partners and at the same time, (coalition leaders) are working hard to teach their soldiers about our cultures," said Afghan Ministry of Defense spokesman, General Mohammed Zaher Azimi, at a September 2012 joint-press conference with British Lt. Gen. Adrian Bradshaw, deputy commander of the International Security Assistance Force.

Bradshaw said coalition forces, too, were getting input from Afghan army, religious, and cultural affairs advisers to add to their cultural training.[19] According to General Azimi, Afghan Army soldiers received *A Brochure for Comprehending the Cultures of the Coalition Forces* to help them understand that the peculiar Westerner behaviors, which had previously sparked fatal outbursts of anger, were not intended to be insulting.

The brochure advised Afghan soldiers that coalition forces consider it normal to share photos of their wives and daughters with friends. Afghans consider it taboo to show outsiders photos of female relatives. Coalition forces might walk in front of people who are praying or point their feet at Afghanis without realizing the anger it might cause. And because blowing their noses in front of others is taboo to Afghanis, they are advised this behavior is not insulting in Western countries.

In his report, Crisis of Trust and Cultural Incompatibility, behavioral and organizational sciences expert, Jeffrey Bordin, warned that cultural misunderstandings frequently provoked Afghani soldiers to shoot U.S. Americans. The report cites a wide array of American behaviors that alienate and infuriate Afghans, such as eating and drinking in front of Afghanis during *Ramadan*; wearing boots when entering mosques; disrespectfully hiding their eyes behind sunglasses when speaking to elders; and throwing gifts to children from moving cars, which is perceived as demeaning instead of generous. Initially, U.S. military officials reportedly ridiculed Bordin's analyses and other cultural disconnects, but eventually accepted them.

Some tragic cultural miscommunications between Iraqis and Americans arose during U.S. military operations in the Iraq War. When Iraqi drivers were ordered to stop at military checkpoints and they didn't, U.S. American soldiers, screening for terrorists and suicide bombers, sometimes fired, injuring or killing innocent Iraqis. The cause of this misperception was simple: the American gesture—raised, straight-arm with open palm forward—

signals "Stop." In Iraq, the same gesture often is interpreted as "Hello."

An Iraqi journalist friend, who was based in Baghdad for the Washington Post, confirmed these press reports and described another heartbreaking scenario. Sometimes, U.S. Marines raised clenched fists at military checkpoints, a signal—to the Marines—that also means "Stop." But to Iraqis and people from some other countries, a clenched fist means "solidarity." As a result, some innocent Iraqi drivers misunderstood this American military gesture, kept driving, and were shot.

Similar misinterpretations have led to deadly consequences, as cultural anthropologist and defense consultant, Montgomery McFate, wrote in *The Military Utility of Understanding Adversary Culture*.[20] When Iraqis converse, they like to be physically very close; in contrast, U.S. Americans habitually prefer a greater interpersonal distance, generally about the length of an out-stretched arm. Marines had to learn that if an Iraqi stands close, it's not necessarily threatening—maybe he just wants to talk. When Iraqis yell and wave their arms vigorously, Americans tend to perceive it as aggressive, while Iraqis hardly notice this since it is normal conversational behavior.

McFate also notes that misperceiving cultural symbols can create unintended, deadly consequences. In Western European tradition, a white flag signifies surrender. So, when Marines saw a black flag, sometimes they assumed it signified ongoing hostilities. However, the Marines misunderstood the intent: many Iraqi Shiites fly black flags from their homes as religious symbols. Tragically, Marines shot some of these homes, suspecting they harbored enemies.

To help troops avoid such cross-cultural mistakes and learn about the cultures of those they're ostensibly assisting, the Pentagon recruited McFate. The database she helped develop gives soldiers information about other cultures—from tribal structures to regional gestures and language quirks. The U.S. Army also assigned social scientists to help combat units navigate perplexing cultural terrains and communicate across cultures.

***

"Every stranger is a blind man."
—Lebanese proverb

Ms. Gillian Gibbons, a newly arrived British teacher at an elementary school in Khartoum, Sudan's capital, told her pupils they would study the behavior of animals. When a seven-year-old girl brought her cuddly brown bear toy to class, Ms. Gibbons invited her students to name the teddy bear. They voted overwhelmingly for Muhammad—the most popular boy's name among the world's Muslims. Police raided the school. Accused of insulting Islam's Prophet, Ms. Gibbons was imprisoned and faced up to six months or a public lashing if found guilty of blasphemy. A seven-year-old defended his British teacher, describing Ms. Gibbons as "very nice." The student said he had suggested calling the teddy bear Muhammad, because it's his own name.[21]

After imams denounced Ms. Gibbons during Friday prayers, about 10,000 people marched through Khartoum, some waving swords and machetes, demanding the blasphemous teacher's execution. Protestors chanted, "Shame, shame on the UK," and "Kill her by firing squad."

While Sudan's top clerics called for the teacher to be severely punished, a Muslim teacher at the Sudanese school, Sudanese Embassy officials in London, and UK Muslim organizations expressed hope the teacher would be released because no harm was intended. Two British Muslim politicians flew to Sudan and convinced President Omar al-Bashir to pardon the teacher. After fifteen days in jail, she returned to Liverpool.

The tale of the teddy bear reveals two mono-dimensional images. Many Islamic fundamentalist Sudanese didn't understand that in Western Christian countries, a teddy bear often is an expression of love and comfort. Conversely, many Westerners didn't understand why Sharia law would forbid linking the Islamic Prophet's name with a stuffed toy animal.

This sharp clash over the teddy bear brings to mind an incident involving an outraged reaction by the then-New York Mayor Giuliani. He accused a British-born painter of Nigerian descent of "disgusting, degenerate Catholic bashing" during an October 8, 1999, interview on Meet the Press, a nationally broadcast U.S. TV news program. The Mayor was reacting to Chris Ofili's "sick" (according to the mayor) painting, Holy Virgin Mary, in an exhibit at the Brooklyn Museum of Art. It depicted a Black Madonna in a blue robe, a traditional attribute of the Virgin Mary. On one bared breast is a lump of dried, varnished elephant dung, and collages resembling butterflies appear to surround the Black Madonna—on closer inspection, they're actually photos of female genitalia from porn magazines.

The provocative mixture of the sacred (Virgin Mary) and the profane (elephant excrement and porn) propelled then-Mayor Giuliani, backed by Catholic leaders, to threaten the Brooklyn Museum of Art. It could either cancel the opening of the show or lose its $7 million annual City grant. As Mayor Giuliani put it, "You don't have a right to a government subsidy for desecrating somebody else's religion."

The artist's defenders pointed out that Ofili, raised as a Roman Catholic, is influenced by African art, which frequently incorporates dung, a symbol of power and fertility in many parts of Africa.[22] Ofili commented that "elephant dung itself is quite a beautiful object," a cultural symbol of regeneration.

Another of his paintings at the Brooklyn Museum exhibit, Afrodizzia, had balls of elephant dung with the names of Miles Davis, Diana Ross, and James Brown written on them. No one accused Ofili of being anti-black.[23] The year before, Ofili won the Turner Prize, the UK's most prestigious prize for contemporary artists. All the art he entered contained his trademark: elephant dung.

Is what the Mayor considered "unholy shit" actually "holy shit"? Maybe so, according to the spirit of this African proverb: "A fruit tree that grows in a dung heap certainly will blossom."

Another passionate conflict over religious icons and symbols arose in a rural-Kentucky Amish community in 2012. Many Amish embrace simple living and shun electricity and modern conveniences such as cars. As a warning to drivers, Kentucky and other U.S. states require the Amish to affix an orange safety triangle on the back of their slow, horse-drawn buggies.[24] This recognized symbol is an important safety alert, especially at night.

But to some strictly observant Amish, the garish orange color conflicts with their sense of modesty. Moreover, the triangle symbol, which to the Amish represents the Holy Trinity, undermines their religion's prohibition against wearing or carrying religious symbols for protection. They believe God, not symbols, will protect them on highways. In this case, two differing perceptions of the triangle eventually were resolved by the Kentucky legislature. It allowed the protesting Amish sect to use reflective tape and lanterns instead of the orange triangle.

In the world of commerce, symbols also have sparked controversy. Puma, the German sportswear company, designed a special shoe with the red, white, and green of the United Arab Emirates' flag to honor the country's 40th birthday, on December 2, 2011. These special SpeedCat shoes were distributed to shops across the UAE. The reaction? Swift and angry: customers were insulted seeing their flag's colors on footwear. In the Muslim world, shoes commonly are considered dirty; showing the bottoms of shoes is an insult.[25] Puma withdrew the shoes and apologized: "The shoe was never intended to upset or offend our customers here in the Middle East, but to give the people of the UAE a piece of locally created design as a symbol of recognition of this great occasion."

"Puma should have borne in mind the cultural sensitivities of the people of the UAE," Abdullah K, an Emirati professional, wrote on CNN's Inside the Middle East blog. "The flag is a very sacred symbol for the UAE. It cannot be trivialized, especially not as footwear." An Arab expatriate working in advertising and marketing, Ramzi Khalaf, told the site: "Big brands have to realize that you cannot have one idea for the whole world. Each area you operate in has to have tailor-made solutions. Especially here in the Middle East, where cultural sensitivities are key, you have to be very careful."

In 2012, a virulently anti-Muslim movie trailer, The Real Life of Muhammad, was posted on YouTube. It provoked large, vehemently anti-US protests throughout much of the Muslim world, including violent attacks on U.S. embassies and consulates. After protests from some Muslim governments, Google, which owns YouTube, voluntarily blocked the twelve-minute video clip in Egypt, Jordan, Libya, Indonesia, Saudi Arabia, Malaysia, India, and Singapore. In September 2012, the Afghani, Bangladeshi, Sudanese, and Pakistani governments blocked YouTube for not removing the video.[26]

The U.S. government condemned the film and tried to make clear that it didn't authorize its production. The Obama administration asked YouTube to review whether to continue hosting the video at all under the company's policies. The American Civil Liberties Union responded: "It does make us nervous when the government throws its weight behind any requests for censorship."

Anger against U.S. American foreign policy aside, one cause of Muslim rage was due to a misunderstanding of U.S. free speech laws. While hate speech is banned and punished in many countries in the developed world, in the U.S. it's protected constitutionally, except if it is likely to produce immediate violence or lawlessness. Through the cultural prism of many in the Muslim world, where strict government censorship of the press and films is common, the U.S. government was ultimately responsible for allowing the production of this controversial film, and its trailer being uploaded to YouTube.

***

We do not see things as they are; we see things as we are."
—Anais Nin

People unaccustomed to seeing veils, whether covering the head, the face, or the entire body, may not understand what veils signify for women who wear them. Whether to ban, encourage, or tolerate the veil, has become a recurrent, controversial topic both in Islamic and non-Islamic countries, particularly after 9/11. Whatever the political issues, there are strong opinions that frequently don't consider different meanings and motivations for veiling, and which may vary from country to country, and individual to individual. While some consider veiling oppressive, others may see it as liberating; while some may suspect a veiled woman is a terrorist, others may see her defying discrimination and ignorance. And what some consider female subjugation, others perceive as an escape from male harassment.

Dr. Lawrence Michalak, a cultural anthropologist and Vice Chair Emeritus of the Center for Middle Eastern Studies at UC Berkeley, explores the wide array of possibilities for misperception in his essay, *The Veil*.

> Sit in a café on any street in Tunis (one of the pleasures of life!), and you will notice that the women passing on the street cover up to different degrees. Those of us who first came to Tunisia in the 1960s recognize this as something new. It is not

a "return" to Islamic dress. Until recently, there was no such thing as women's Islamic dress in Tunisia.

In the 1960s and earlier there was a garment called the *safsari*—a long white rectangle of cloth that some women wore over their clothing. However, the *safsari* had no religious meaning. It was a sign that the woman was urban rather than rural. Rural women wore brightly colored, loose fitting clothing appropriate for work in the fields, and most women, rural and urban, wore Western-style dress, which is still the case. Nowadays, the *safsari* has almost disappeared.

In the 1970s a new form of women's dress began to appear—the headscarf—sometimes accompanied by a smock-like dress that covered the woman's shoulders and arms. Tunisians called it the hijab, Arabic for "veil," although it really doesn't veil very much—mainly the hair, and sometimes only partially. In Tunisia in the 1990s, President Ben Ali (who fled the country in January 2011) banned the headscarf in schools and government offices, and the police sometimes harassed women wearing the headscarf, but the ban was never strictly enforced.

Veiling in Tunisia continues to be a widespread topic of conversation and analysis. Some scholars started counting the percentage of Tunisian women in different cities and towns who wore headscarves. Veiling (their argument went) meant that the woman wearing the covering was a conservative Muslim, and if a high percentage of women in a particular place veiled, it meant that particular place was more religiously conservative.

However, there are problems with this argument. To begin with, veiling is a question of degree. A woman might wear a headscarf that doesn't completely cover her hair, or she might cover all of her hair, or all of her hair and her neck as well. She might wear a sleeveless dress, or a dress that covers her arms. Some women wear gloves and long socks. Very few women cover up fully—such as the Saudi *nikab*, which masks the face and even the eyes.

Also, what does one make of a Tunisian woman with a headscarf accompanied by a low-cut dress that shows lots of bosom, with bare arms and lots of leg? This seems like a contradiction. When I asked about this, a Tunisian male friend told me that it means, "I'm a morally strict young woman and you won't get any physical intimacy from me...but when I get married my husband is going to have lots of fun!"

A Tunisian woman journalist suggested, in an article in *Jeune Afrique*, that fashion is the most important reason for veiling. Most women wear the veil as they would a miniskirt—because it's the fashion—and the cut and the color are what are important to them. Many of the women who veil have never read the Quran or performed the prayer. Some go veiled during the week and then wear bikinis to the beach on the weekend. Some wear the veil to nightclubs with whisky-drinking boyfriends. The journalist pointed out that the veil is found more in Tunis than in outlying areas, and she speculated that new fashions—such as the headscarf—come later to rural Tunisia.

Head coverings vary from culture to culture and from one historical era to the next. In the U.S., until about the middle of the 1900s, every self-respecting man wore a head covering. Remember Frank Sinatra? He almost always wore a hat, well into the second-half of the century. Until the late 1950s, college men at UC Berkeley wore head coverings that indicated what year in school they were—for example, freshmen wore "beanies" and seniors wore "pugs."

In the end, you can't tell much from how people are dressed. Just as you can't judge a book by its cover, neither can you judge a woman by her clothing—or a man, for that matter. I have known traditionally dressed men with very modern ideas, and men in Western suits who would feel right at home with the Taliban.

It is true that a headscarf can be a religious statement, but this is not always so. Nowhere in the Quran is there a requirement that women (other than the wives of the Prophet) must veil. Instead, the Quran stipulates that both women and men dress modestly. Since Islam is a universal religion, and since what is "modest" varies from culture to culture, this means that acceptable dress varies. In Saudi Arabia, modest dress means that Muslim women must cover completely. In Iran they must cover almost completely. But these are local interpretations of modesty, and they are cultural, rather than religious.

In most Muslim countries, such as Tunisia, there is a broad range of permissible dress for women. In

Saudi Arabia and Iran—and in France and Turkey—there is not. In France, Muslim women are not free to wear veils in public. In Turkey, a woman with a headscarf was not allowed to take her seat in the parliament, even though she had been democratically elected to office.

Here are ten possible reasons—other than religion—why a Tunisian woman might wear a headscarf:

1. I do it to annoy my parents, especially my mother, who tells me that her generation abandoned covering.

2. On TV, I saw some women in Egypt who wear it, and I think it looks great!

3. I want a man to love me for my character and my mind, not for my body.

4. I just washed my hair, and I can't do a thing with it.

5. My family is poor, and I can't afford nice clothes, but I don't want people to see.

6. When I wear a headscarf, the guys on the bus tend to leave me alone.

7. I want people to think that I'm a virgin so that I can find a husband more easily.

8. I'm so beautiful that I have to cover up to keep the guys from going crazy.

9. I'm self-conscious about being unattractive, so I leave my looks to people's imagination.

And, finally:

10. It's cold out today and I want to keep my head warm.

In other words, sometimes a headscarf is just a headscarf!

****

"We know remarkably little about each other."
—Police officer, referring to
the U.S. American Sikh community

Just as a woman wearing a veil may be stereotyped as a terrorist or terrorist-sympathizer, some people associate a bearded, turban-wearing man as an Osama Bin Laden supporter. Sikh men commonly wear turbans and beards, a sign they were baptized in their religion, one that is distinct from Islam. In the West, Sikhs are largely misunderstood—even though their religion is the world's fifth largest, and there are over half a million U.S. American Sikhs. Since 9/11, there have been hundreds of violent attacks on Sikh Americans and on their temples.[27]

Because of the attacks, intimidation, and harassment of Sikhs in America, the U.S. Department of Justice and the Sikh American Legal Defense Fund produced a training video, in 2007, *On Common Ground: Sikh American Cultural Competency Training for Law Enforcement*. The video explains how to treat a Sikh man with respect and cultural sensitivity.

The Sikh turban represents Sikh identity and dignity and shouldn't be touched or removed by law enforcement or security at airports. Rather, the man should remove his own turban in a private space and be offered a clean cloth to cover his hair. Because hair is considered sacred, most Sikh men don't cut their hair or beards. In hospitals, Sikh men have panicked when uninformed doctors or nurses try to shave their body hair before an angiogram.

At airports, officials have been alarmed to discover Sikh males carrying "daggers." The *kirpan*, a ceremonial dagger, is an article of faith, which must be worn at all times as a symbolic reminder that Sikhs must struggle against injustice. The video advises law officers to request that Sikhs put their *kirpans* inside their checked luggage.

In 2014, of the half-million active and reserve U.S. Army troops, only three were Sikhs, because U.S. military policy against long hair and beards presents some challenges. "I would gladly sacrifice my life for the mission," said Maj. Kamaljeet Singh Kalsi, who, in 2009, was the first Sikh allowed into the Army in decades, "but I could not cut my hair and remove my turban. They're not mine to give. They belong to my God."

During his service, Major Kalsi kept his beard knotted to allow space to fasten his gas mask and wore a special camouflaged "diamond-shaped turban" made from Army uniform cloth. "It took a little maneuvering," he told the Los Angeles Times. Sometimes his different appearance was useful, he said, recalling being in a doctor's tent in Afghanistan when locals "felt a little more comfortable around me... Maybe it was the turban and beard." He was awarded a Bronze Star for his service in Afghanistan.

Sikh efforts to prod the White House and Pentagon to grant faster religious exemptions have strong Congressional backing. Still, the military's grooming policies "are an integral part of unit cohesion, good order and discipline and, ultimately, mission accomplishment," according to Army Spokeswoman Alayne Conway. Recruits must wear "neat and conservative" hairstyles, with a "tapered" cut, and a clean-shaven face. Mustaches are allowed. U.S. courts have affirmed the military's right to place unit cohesion and morale over the rights of recruits to express their religion.

In 2013, the U.S. Defense Department issued new guidelines on granting religious exemptions for Sikhs and others. Sikhs complain the new policy makes things worse, because a Sikh must cut off his hair and beard while awaiting a response to his religious exemption request. Even if it's granted, before every new assignment he has to reapply for an exemption—and face the possibility of being required to cut his hair and beard.

For practicing Sikhs like Harpreet Singh, it's not acceptable. Singh recalls arriving at Fort Jackson, South Carolina, for training. A drill sergeant mocked his turban and pulled him aside, assuming he was a translator, not a soldier. Another sergeant pressured him to cut his hair and shave his beard, saying he should make "sacrifices" to join the Army. Singh's request for religious exemption was rejected. Singh left the Army before getting into boot camp.[28]

While American Sikhs are pushing the U.S. government to do more to let them serve, the Canadian, British, and Indian armed services enlist Sikh soldiers—they don't regard beards and turbans as undermining military *esprit de corps.* In fact, Sikhs have been serving in the British military for over 150 years.

One Sikh sees joining the U.S. Army as very much about becoming an American. Yet, while working as a UPS driver, he often was confronted by customers who called the police when he was delivering packages. He printed up T-shirts with a response: "I am a Sikh. Google It."[29]

Like Sikh Americans, some Hindu Americans, also with ancestral roots in India, have had controversial encounters with other Americans because of differing perceptions of what is sacred. Many Hindus live near Kennedy Airport in Queens, New York; Jamaica Bay reminds some of them of the sacred Ganges River in India. To celebrate festivals, from births to weddings and deaths, they put religious offerings to Mother Ganga, the goddess of the rivers, into Jamaica Bay. The ritual offerings—cremation ashes, incense, flowers, fruit, saris, even statues—help cleanse the soul, remove sickness, pain, and suffering, and ensure blessings in this life and the next. Yet, to other residents, and national park rangers in the area, the offerings are debris that is polluting Jamaica Bay, damaging a fragile ecosystem enjoyed by picnickers, fishermen, and kayakers.[30]

When religious Hindus are told they can't throw their "trash" into the Bay, their religious feelings are violated. Dispersing cremated human remains on holy water is an ancient Hindu ritual, required to pass to the next life of reincarnation successfully. Some new religious immigrants are unaware of the regulations, others refuse to abandon the sacred ritual, but some find ways to honor their traditions without violating U.S. American rules.

Efforts to reconcile two divergent views of Jamaica Bay advanced because of an important shared value: respecting the earth. Groups of Hindu Americans helped park rangers clean up the shoreline. A former park ranger visited dozens of Hindu temples, explaining that offerings can strangle the sea, choke birds, and disrupt the food chain. As a result, many Hindus now come to Jamaica Bay to pray with their offerings and then take them home. To honor Hindu traditions, in 2014, the Queens Museum ran an exhibit, "Sacred Waters: A Collection of Hindu Offerings from Jamaica Bay."[31]

***

"Do not have greater respect for money than for man."
—Vietnamese saying

"Respect is given to wealth, not to men."
—Lebanese saying

From dawn to dusk, elderly Koreans, some with walkers, wheelchairs, and canes, sipped coffee or shared French fries at a McDonald's in Queens, New York. Then, in January 2014, police ordered them out. According to McDonald's, the battle started because, for five years, Koreans gathered at tables for hours refusing to let other customers sit. "It's a McDonald's, not a senior center," said the manager, who called the police after the group refused to budge, and other customers asked for refunds because there was nowhere to sit. The seniors were violating McDonald's twenty-minute dining limit.

The older Koreans say they're loyal patrons, entitled to meet and linger. Many are lonely, widowed, and on tight budgets, and are attracted by McDonald's proximity, prices, and the companionship. With no senior center within walking distance, McDonald's, with its large windows, is good for socializing and people watching. The Golden Arches became their inexpensive home away from home.

The septuagenarian situation escalated. Each time police ousted the entrenched men and women, they simply walked around the block—and returned. Proud, independent, and defiant, elderly Koreans continued arriving, staging a de facto sit-in. Many in the Korean community were outraged, seeing their senior citizens treated as criminal space-hogs, rather than as highly respected elders. As a result, in January 2014, Korean community leaders urged a worldwide McDonald's boycott for a month. The news made headlines, even in Seoul.

Local politicians, led by a Korean-American New York State Assemblyman, brokered a compromise that promoted respect for both seniors and businesses in the area. McDonald's allowed the Koreans extended seating privileges, except during crowded peak hours between 11 a.m. and 3 p.m. Senior centers in the area provided transportation to and from the restaurant. And McDonald's employees agreed not to call the police to resolve possible future conflicts.[32]

In Los Angeles, another contrasting perception of what "respect" means caused difficulties. During the 1980s and 90s, many mom-and-pop stores in poor, inner-city African-American communities were owned and operated by Korean immigrants. These shopkeepers complained about loud-talking, cursing, African-American customers. The teenagers, especially, were perceived as not showing respect for older Korean merchants.

From the point of view of many African-Americans, they were ignored as customers when they entered the store—it was obvious because the Korean merchants didn't greet them or even smile. In addition, many African-Americans didn't understand that in Korean culture, smiling, making eye contact, and engaging in small talk with strangers is impolite, inappropriate, and even bizarre. Often, these immigrants spoke limited English. Friction intensified in the economically depressed neighborhood.[33]

Instead of handing African-American customers their change, most Korean merchants just placed the money on the counter. According to Korean etiquette, this practice is the most polite. Yet African-Americans perceived it as rude and dehumanizing.

Cultural misunderstandings and culture clashes exacerbated. Perceiving Korean-American merchants as "economic exploiters," some African-Americans residents called for boycotts of Korean-run groceries, liquor stores, restaurants, and laundries. On April 29, 1992, relations between Korean-American and African-American communities in Los Angeles exploded into rioting, looting, and killing—partially fuelled by differences in cultural and linguistic styles.[34]

For six-days, African-American rioters targeted Korean-immigrant-owned stores. To prevent looters and arsonists from mistaking their shops as Korean-owned, many black business owners displayed "black-owned" signs in front of their stores. In all, 2,280 Korean-American businesses were looted or burned, with $400 million in property damage. A few days later, on April 29, 1992, more than 30,000 Korean-Americans in Los Angeles came together for a "Peace March," the largest gathering in Asian-American history.

The Korean-American community remembers the Los Angeles riots as a key historical event, and a catalyst for examining cultural misunderstandings, language barriers, and Korean-immigrant unfamiliarity with aspects of U.S. American society.

Both Korean-American merchants and African-American customers realized how dependent they were on each other. With so many burned-out Korean stores, African-American residents had to walk miles just to buy basic necessities. Korean merchants realized that they had to reach out more and become part of the local community. Both Korean-immigrant merchants and African-American customers became more courteous to one another. Cross-cultural awareness and behavioral changes helped ease tensions between the two groups.

Ideas about how respect is perceived across cultures is illustrated in an exchange that took place during an official visit of a U.S. delegation to China in 1978, shortly after US-Chinese diplomatic relations reopened. While touring an important Beijing cemetery, one U.S. American delegate noticed oranges placed on many gravesites. Jokingly, he asked the Chinese guide, "When will your ancestors come up to eat the oranges?" The guide paused and then, clearly irritated, answered: "When your ancestors come up to smell the flowers!"

* * *

"Because each of us has something someone else lacks, and because we each lack something someone else has, we gain by interaction."
—Jonathan Sacks, *The Dignity of Difference*

Lack of meaningful contact between people from different cultures is a major source of misperception. Face-to-face interactions between people with different values and worldviews are essential tools for bridging cultural differences and humanizing the "other." The experience of other cultures, and understanding other ways of perceiving the world, are two major things I learned during my years in Kenya as a Peace Corps Volunteer. These ideas have been reinforced by working in the field of international people-to-people educational exchange.

After the 2015 Charlie Hebdo and kosher market murders, a French sociologist joined over one-and-a-half-million people in Paris for the *Je Suis Charlie* solidarity march. Seeing a man holding a *Quran* in one hand and a copy of Charlie Hebdo magazine in the other, she felt hope. "Polarization can only be diffused when we learn to talk across our differences without blaming each other."

With the alarming increase of political, religious, and ethnic polarization around the world—often fueled by instantaneous, faceless technology—I think of Bussy Saint George, only 18 miles from Paris. For four centuries it was a village, with one Roman Catholic church. Today, it's a "planned city" with 25,000 residents, mostly immigrants from former French colonies in North and West Africa, the Caribbean, China, Laos, and elsewhere.

To meet their needs, Mayor Hugues Rondeau, a practicing Catholic, had an idea: a cluster of faiths. Catholics have joined Muslims, Jews, Buddhists, and Protestants in planning a sprawling Esplanade of the Religions. Imagine a mosque next to a synagogue, a Laotian Buddhist pagoda, and an enormous Taiwanese Buddhist temple. It's a bold initiative, especially in France, where principles of secularism are intended, sometimes unsuccessfully, to foster a sense of common French identity. Yet, community members have multiple cultural and religious identities, and without paths to mutual understanding, they're in danger of clashing.

The Esplanade of the Religions aspires to be a "laboratory of tolerance" and "interfaith dialogue," where people of all faiths will be encouraged to visit each other's houses of worship, as the Mayor puts it. The large mosque, designed around a courtyard, has a cultural center and a prayer hall, open to all. "We're for cohabitation" with other religions, including the Jews, whose synagogue will go up next-door, local Muslim leader Farid Chaoui told the New York Times, "and we're very optimistic."[35]

So, too, is the local rabbi, Guy Benarousse, who's often asked whether Muslims and Jews can get along. "To show everyone that living together is a nonevent, it's a beautiful thing," said Benarousse, an Algerian Jew, "here, we're going to show everyone how to live together." Benarousse wants the community to reflect the one he left in Algeria: Jews and Muslims living side-by-side. "As a symbol, I asked that the mosque be built next door to the synagogue. The point is to say, 'We can disagree, but we have to talk to each other.'"

Farid Chaoui, vice president of the Muslim Community Association, agrees. "There have been no problems—on the contrary, Jews and Muslims, especially in North Africa, lived for centuries together." Chaoui, also from Algeria, added that he and Benarousse often "joke that we're cousins."[36]

In this unusual multi-faith experiment, Buddhists and Muslims attended a Jewish tree-planting holiday at the site of the future synagogue. The Catholic priest attended a Lunar New Year service at the Taiwanese Buddhist Temple. "All the religions here, all of us are good friends," said the temple's head nun.

Some residents, however, have misgivings, deriding the Esplanade of the Religions as a religious theme park in the image of nearby Disneyland Paris. Could this bold initiative serve as a model for mutual understanding and multi-faith cooperation in France, which seems to be experiencing growing intolerance toward religious and racial minorities?

The Esplanade of the Religions encourages people to humanize each other and reminds me of International House. The late Richard Newton, a former resident, and, later, Dean of UC Berkeley's College of Engineering, eloquently expressed its principles. In the aftermath of 9/11, he shared these remarks with the International House community:

> Now, as I listen to the national debate and hear many people express their anger and frustration, while others coolly speak of retribution and revenge, I find myself drawing deeply upon one of the greatest gifts Berkeley International House has given me. While CNN projects maps of the world, where countries are represented by colors within boundaries and commentators speak of nations and

peoples as categories, with an implication of a common view and a shared responsibility, I can only see faces—many of these faces are from my time under this roof. Pakistan is Abid and Rashid. India is Asha. Turkey is Can. Germany is Horst. Israel is Natan. Iran is Massoud. Ghana is Kofi. France is Michele, and Japan is Hiro. These are all real individuals to me, people I laughed with, people I cried with, and people I disagreed with over a myriad of issues. But in the end, these people were my friends, and they became a part of my family.

The spirit of these remarks was echoed when Shashi Tharoor, former UN Under Secretary General, shared this ancient Indian story with the World Affairs Council of Northern California:

The Sage asks his disciples: "When does the night end?"

And the disciples answer: "Why, dawn, of course."

The Sage says: "I know that, but when does the night end, and the dawn begin?"

So the first disciple, who's from the hot and tropical south, says: "Oh, I know. It's when the first streaks of sunlight illuminate the palm on the coconut trees swaying gently in the breeze. That's when the night ends, and the dawn begins!"

The Sage says: "No, my son."

He turns to the second disciple, who's from the cold and snowy north.

The disciple says: "I know. It's when the streaks of sunlight glint off the snow and ice of the mountaintops of the Himalayas. That's when the night ends, and the dawn begins!"

The Sage says: "No, my sons. It's when two travelers from the farthest ends of our world meet and embrace each other as brothers. It's when they realize they sleep under the same sky, see the same stars, and dream the same dreams. That is when the night ends, and the dawn begins."

Questions and Activities, Chapter Five

1. As in the example of a child sleeping in the same bed as his parents and eating from their hands, many cultural values and behaviors are typically shaped in the formative years. Interview a parent from a different country than yours who has been in your country for at least six months to a year. What has the parent observed about child rearing practices, from babies to teenagers, in your country that differ from his or her country? What do these differences suggest about contrasting values in the two countries, or between you and your interviewee? What are some of the positive aspects of the two approaches that may not have been initially perceived or considered by you or your interviewee?

2. Look for culture clashes reflected in news of the day. Consider, for example, conflicts in the worlds of business, diplomacy, ethnicity, war or religion. In what respects might any one or more of the conflicts

selected be rooted in cultural differences and an inability of either or both parties to understand or see the underlying intentions of the other party? Interview individuals who come from cultural backgrounds reflected in both sides of the conflict. Ask each individual what the meaning might be and/or intention of the behavior which the other side may misunderstand.

3. Log on to your *Cultural Detective Online* subscription and open the *Islam* Package. Begin your exploration by clicking on the Overview tab and review the "Introduction to Islam" section, as well as the various sections under the Supplementary Material tab, especially the section entitled, "Sensitive Issues That May Arise," while considering Chapter Five's discussion of the veil. Then go to the Incidents tab and click on "Prayer Time Issues." Fill in the top quadrants of the *Cultural Detective* Worksheet and compare your perceptions of the critical incident with those of the Muslim immigrants and the U.S. American workers. Now, with an understanding of the various perspectives in play, how would you propose to bridge the differences in a manner that would bring the conflict to an end in a mutually acceptable fashion? Note your proposed Bridges in the Worksheet. Compare your answers with the Author Ideas and discuss your proposed solutions with individuals of Muslim and non-Muslim backgrounds.

4. For additional perspectives on the meanings of symbols across cultures as illustrated in Chapter Five, log on to your *Cultural Detective Online* subscription and open the *Global Business Ethics* Package. Click on

the Incidents tab and go to "Offensive Symbolism." Review the incident and complete the Worksheet. Compare your perceptions of the swastika with those of Phillip and the Indian office. Considering the actual source of the conflict, how would you propose to resolve the issue? Compare your proposal with that of the Author Ideas in the Cultural Bridges section. Then, review Additional Debrief notes on "Offensive Symbolism" in the Supplementary Material. To explore additional perspectives and sensitivities about the swastika, log on to the *Jewish Culture* Package and go to the "Vandalism" incident. Fill in that Worksheet, and then compare your reactions to the incident with those of the Jewish parents and the non-Jewish school principal and administration. Discuss your proposed solutions to the conflict with someone of Jewish heritage and someone who has had little or no contact with Jewish people.

Notes

1. James Hookway, "Ikea's Products Make Shoppers Blush in Thailand," *The Wall Street Journal*, June 5, 2012.

2. *Ibid.*

3. Ashante Infantry, "Ikea, what's Swedish for Oops?" *Toronto Star*, June 6, 2012.

4. "Buick Masturbation Car Renamed," *BBC News*, October 23, 2003.

5. Larry Claasen, "Choosing the Right Brand Name," *Financial Mail*, July 18, 2013.

6. "Advertising Pitfalls," *The Mercury* (South Africa), January 21, 2013.

7. Ishaan Tharoor, "Belgian Chocolate Company is Latest to Decide ISIS Might Not be Such a Good Name," *The Washington Post*, October 24, 2014.

8. Sarah Boesveld, "They've Distorted My Name," *Globe and Mail*, February 11, 2010.

9. Michael Kilean, "U.S. Planning to Bar 'Guests' from Controls," *Chicago Tribune*, February 23, 2001.

10. Vicki Viotti, "Ehime Maru Lessons Shared," *Honolulu Advertiser*, July 27, 2004.

11. Erik Eckholm, "Collison in China," *The New York Times*, April 4, 2001.

12. Sharon LaFraniere, "Chinese, But Not Their Leaders, Flock to U.S. Envoy," *The New York Times*, November 11, 2011.

13. Terrence McCoy, "Gumchew Diplomacy," *The Washington Post*, November 12, 2014.

14. "Bill Gate's Handshake with S. Korea's Park Sparks Debate," NPR, April 23, 2013.

15. "Bill Gates 'Disrespects' S. Korean President," *The Telegraph*, April 23, 2013.

16. Paul Beckett, "On Norway, The Media and A Family's Tragedy," *The Wall Street Journal*, March 20, 2012.

17. Mohammad Asif, "West Bengal: Kids in Custody Row Given to Mother," *Hindustan Times*, January 8, 2013.

18. Rod Norland, "In Afghanistan, Avoiding Violent Misunderstandings Among Troops," *The New York Times*, September 6, 2012.

19. Heath Druzin, "Afghans Create 'Western Culture' Manual to Help Counter Insider Attacks," *Stars and Stripes*, September 6 & 12, 2012.

20. Montgomery McFate, "The Military Utility of Understanding Adversary Culture," *Joint Force Quarterly*, July, 2005.

21. Xan Rice and Andrew Heavens, "Pupil Defends Teacher in Muhammad Teddy Furor," *The Guardian*, November 27, 2007.

22. Carol Vogel, "Chris Ofili Holds Fast to His Inspiration," *The New York Times*, September 28, 1999.

23. Michael Kimmelman, "Of Dung and Its Many Meanings in the Art World," *The New York Times*, October 5, 1999.

24. Steve Eder, "Amish Bridle at Buggy Rules," *The Wall Street Journal*, March 16, 2012.

25. "Puma Apologizes and Pulls Flag from Shoes and Shelves in the UAE Amid Criticism," *Associated Press*, November 30, 2011.

26. Karin Bruillard, "Pakistan Blocks YouTube After Shutdown of Facebook over Mohammed Issue," *The Washington Post*, May 21, 2010.

27. Ethan Bronner, "Mourning Victims Sikhs Lament Being Mistaken for Radicals or Militants," *The New York Times*, August 6, 2012.

28. Lalita Clozel, "U.S. Sikhs Say Military's Ban on Long Hair and Beards Keeps Them Out," *Los Angeles Times*, April 13, 2014.

29. James Dao, "Taking on Rules to Ease Sikh's Path to the Army," *The New York Times*, July 8, 2013.

30. Sam Dolnick, "Hindus Find a Ganges in Queens, To Park Rangers' Dismay," *The New York Times*, April 21, 2011.

31. Lisa Colangelo, "New Film Examines Hindu Rituals Held at Jamaica Bay," *New York Daily News*, June 20, 2014.

32. Palash Ghosh, "McDonald's vs. elderly Koreans in Queens, New York," *International Business Times*, February 3, 2014.

33. Benjamin Bailey, "Communicative Behavior and Conflict Between African-American Customers and Korean retailers in Los Angeles," *Discourse and Society*, Sage Journals, January, 2000.

34. Itabari Njeri, "Swapping Lessons: In Black-Korean Conflict," *Los Angeles Times*, January 11, 1990.

35. Scott Sayre, "Bucking French Tradition, City Sets Up a Kind of Holy Quarter," *The New York Times*, April 3, 2013.

36. Anne Cohen, "Could Run-Of-the Mill French Suburb be Global Model?" *Jewish Daily Forward*, May 10, 2013.

CHAPTER SIX

Misperceptions: Maxims and Musings from Around the World

My years as a Peace Corps Volunteer in Kenya, and work in West Africa, made me aware of my own cultural blinders. I'd been like a child who, seeing wild birds for the first time in New York's Central Park, asks, "Mommy, where are their cages?" My mind-opening adventures in Africa pushed me out of my cultural cage and taught me to fly. But, after returning to the U.S., many of my American friends couldn't understand my stories, or the awakenings I'd undergone in Africa. In time, I realized that they were unable to see beyond their own cultural prisms.

That's when I started collecting proverbs and observations from wise people around the world. They helped friends understand my experiences. As a Talmudic rabbi observed centuries ago, *"A quotation at the right moment is like bread in a famine."*

The following musings and maxims about perception and perspective are offered in the spirit of this Ethiopian saying: *"A proverb is to speech, what salt is to food."*

> *You don't really see the world if you only look through your own window.* —Ukrainian
>
> *What you see in yourself is what you see in the world.* —Afghani
>
> *Go as far as you can see, and when you get there, you'll see further.* —Persian

"In the West, when you fail to describe, things fail to exist. In the East, when you fail to describe, things emerge." —Kunio Kundo

"No man ever looks at the world with pristine eyes. He sees it edited by a definite set of customs, institutions and ways of thinking." —Ruth Benedict

The stranger sees only what he knows. —Dogon, West Africa

"What the eyes see and the ears hear, the mind believes." —Harry Houdini

"As I am, so I see." —Ralph Waldo Emerson

Everyone is kneaded out of the same dough, but not baked in the same oven. —Yiddish

"Every man takes the limit of his own field of vision for the limits of the world." —Arthur Schopenhauer

A blind person who sees is better than a seeing person who is blind. —Persian

"The question is not what you look at, but what you see." —Henry David Thoreau

The eye shuns what it does not see. —Irish

The eye is blind if the mind is absent. —Italian

Love is blind, so you have to feel your way. —Brazilian

"The voyage of discovery is not in seeing new landscapes, but in having new eyes." —Marcel Proust

Self-Deception

Remember the first time you heard your voice on a recording? Like me, you probably didn't think it sounded like you. When I replayed a radio interview I had done, I didn't recognize my own voice. Have you been startled at how you appear in photos and videos? Too fat? Hideous hair? Bags under your eyes? Just as we don't hear our voices as others hear them, often we don't see ourselves as others see us. Here are some observations about self-deception from various cultures:

He who smells bad does not know it himself. —Japanese

Everyone thinks his own spit tastes good. —Persian

A camel does not see its hump. —Arabic

Eyes can see everything, except themselves. —Serbo-Croatian

You cannot see the mountain when you are on it. —Chinese

Ever overhear an Italian describing how her foreign host overcooked pasta? How a Honolulu waitress refers to a non-tipping Japanese customer? Wonder how your marriage appears to your Ethiopian houseguest? Outsiders often see things that are hidden to those closest to the situation. Consider these reflections:

A guest sees more in an hour than the host sees in a year. —Polish

If you want to know what water is like, don't ask a fish. —Chinese

Abroad one has a hundred eyes; at home, not one. —German

There are men who walk through woods and see no trees. —Mongolian

The Mongolian proverb above was illustrated when I asked two friends to interpret this psychological puzzle:

A young boy and his father were in a terrible car accident. The father was killed and the son was very seriously injured. An ambulance rushed them to the hospital, where the father was pronounced dead. The son, who was seriously injured, was hurried into surgery. Just before the surgery was to begin, the surgeon looked down at the boy and exclaimed: "I can't operate on this boy; he's my son!"

We asked friends who the surgeon was. The wife, a prominent M.D., a hematologist and oncologist in New York, didn't know. Puzzled, she looked at her husband, a professor of intercultural business. He also was stumped. I told them the answer, which is hidden in plain sight: the surgeon was the boy's mother.

Though the modest number of female surgeons in the U.S. is increasing, when people are asked this question—including females—most don't know the answer. Because few of us think of surgeons as being women, our "flawed" perception can blind us to reality.

Context Often Is Everything

During discussions about stereotypes in my intercultural classes, I ask students to describe a "skinhead." They say "shaved head," "boots," "leather," and "tattoos," and throw out negative words like "angry," "violent," "racist," "neo-Nazi," and "white supremacist." I tell them to imagine a tattooed skinhead running toward a well-dressed businessman with a briefcase and umbrella. I ask them to guess what the skinhead is about to do. Most students say he is about to "attack and rob" the businessman.

Then I show them a YouTube video ad sponsored by the *Guardian* newspaper. It shows a skinhead running toward a businessman, and then we see he is about to be crushed by a load of falling bricks. Suddenly, we see the skinhead pulling the businessman to safety.

The video shows the importance of trying to look at things through other's eyes. As Harper Lee wrote in *To Kill A Mocking Bird*, "You never really understand a person until you consider things from his point of view." Context and perspective are essential for understanding realities different from own our experiences.

In the land of the naked, people are ashamed of clothes. —Livonian, Latvia, and Estonia

Do not think there are no crocodiles because the water is calm. —African

Night hides a world but reveals a universe. —Persian

When one always drinks vinegar, one does not know anything sweeter exists. —Yiddish

Don't expect to be offered a chair when you visit a place where the chief himself sits on the floor.
—Ghanaian

"An enemy is one whose story we have not heard."
—Gene Knudson Hoffman

Last winter, the heater at my gym broke. The gym was so chilly that I spent extra time warming up on the treadmill. Ten days later, the gym felt unusually hot. Obviously, the heater had been repaired, but the temperature was unbearable. This is a gym, I thought, not a sauna. I checked the thermostat: 68 degrees Fahrenheit, exactly as it had been before the heater broke. But I'd become so accustomed to the unheated gym that the normal temperature seemed abnormal.

That temperature experience reminded me of Mark Twain's wise observation: *"When I was a boy of fourteen, my father was so ignorant that I could hardly stand to have the old man around. But when I got to be twenty-one, I was astonished at how much the old man had learned in seven years."*

These sayings illustrate the important perspectives that comparisons can offer:

I wept because I had no shoes, until I saw a man who had no feet. —Persian

Bad is never good until worse happens. —Danish

"What the caterpillar calls the end, the rest of the world calls a butterfly." —Lao-tzu

When the moon is not full, the stars shine more brightly. —Buganda, Uganda

In a flat country, a hill thinks itself a mountain. —Kurdish

Fear and love make everything bigger. —Spanish

"Forty is the old age of youth. Fifty is the youth of old age." —Victor Hugo

"We live in a moment of history where change is so speeded up that we begin to see the present only when it is already disappearing." —R.D. Laing

"History is the present. That's why every generation writes it anew." —E.L. Doctorow

Character: Like tea bags, you don't know what's inside until it's placed in hot water. —source unknown

Perspectives on "Truth"

Pascal once observed that, *"The truths on this side of the Pyrenees are falsehoods on the other."* The wisdom in his words was clear when I ate in restaurants on both the French side of the Pyrenees, which generally welcome dogs, and on the Spanish side, which usually discourage them.

During cross-cultural training sessions in Silicon Valley for women in high tech from various Middle Eastern and African countries, we discussed how, in some cultures, dogs are considered dirty and are not allowed in homes. In some cultures, dog meat is a delicacy, and in others, dogs are treated like valued family members. A Nigerian computer programmer described her surprise at seeing slick TV ads for dog food, and supermarkets that had more rows of dog food than baby food. I answered that in San Francisco, dogs outnumber children. "You're joking," an Egyptian software developer said. "That can't be true."

It is true, I answered. A woman from Algeria was stunned to see the Wag Hotel for dogs near the San Francisco Airport. We Googled it and found out that owners can drop off their dogs 24/7/365. There are three Wag Hotels in California, and guests (canine and feline) can have a variety of rooms, suites, meal plans, grooming, play activities—and training, at the hotel's Wag University. Traveling owners even can watch Wag Cam to see their happy pets. And when owners retrieve their pets, they can buy matching pajamas for all family members, including dogs and cats, from Pajamagram.

"Why are you Americans so crazy about your pets, when some children don't have enough to eat?" asked a woman from Rwanda who'd witnessed genocide. These are only anecdotes, I emphasized, not the full picture. They certainly don't reveal how all U.S. Americans feel about dogs and cats. I'm allergic to cats; my wife is afraid of dogs.

When these women return to their homes in the Middle East and Africa, I wonder if they'll retell the Wag Hotel story, and if so, how accurately? Whether people pamper dogs or eat them as food, it's worth reflecting on the nature of truth. "There is no truth," observed Gustave Flaubert, "there is only perception."

The truth has many faces. —Yiddish

"In this deceptive world, what is true or false depends on the color of the eyes through which we look."
—Ramon de Campoamor

What is true by lamplight is not always true by sunlight. —French

A fish gets bigger when it gets away. —Japanese.

Until the lions have their historians, tales of the hunt shall always glorify the hunter. —Nigerian

"I don't exaggerate; I just remember big."
—Mark Twain

If you add to the truth, you take something away from it. —Hebrew

"It isn't so astonishing the number of things I remember as the number of things I remember that just ain't so." —Mark Twain

"As a general rule, if you want to get to the truth, hear both sides and believe neither." —Josh Billings

"The pure and simple truth is rarely pure and never simple." —Oscar Wilde

To believe is easier than investigation. —Serbian

"Man prefers to believe what he prefers to be true."
—Francis Bacon

On Dogma and Uncertainty

We often cling to our beliefs as if they are universal truths. As Andre Gide once wrote, *"Believe those who are seeking the truth; doubt those who find it."* Twentieth century philosopher Isaiah Berlin described the unspeakable dangers of a one-dimensional dogmatic worldview this way:

> One belief more than any is responsible for the slaughter of individuals. It is the belief that those who do not share my faith or my race or my ideology do not share my humanity—that at most they are second-class citizens. If faith is what makes us human, then those who do not share my faith are less than fully human. From this equation flowed the Crusades, the Inquisitions, the jihads, the pogroms, the Holocaust—the blood of human sacrifice through the ages.

It is good to understand we don't necessarily hold the truth, often only our particular perspective or bias.

* * *

"Dogma does not mean the absence of thought, but the end of thought." —Gilbert Chesterton

"Convictions are more dangerous enemies of truth than lies." —Fredrich Nietzche

To be uncertain is to be uncomfortable, but to be certain is to be ridiculous. —Chinese

He who knows nothing, doubts nothing. —Brazilian

"To be certain: to be mistaken at the top of one's voice." —Ambrose Bierce

"Frantic orthodoxy is never rooted in faith, but in doubt. It is when we are unsure that we are doubly sure." —Reinhold Niebuhr

"A fanatic is one who sticks to his guns whether they are loaded or not." —Franklin P. Jones

"From fanaticism to barbarism is only one brief step." —Diderot

"A tree that cannot bend will crack in the wind." —Lao-tzu

"Impiety: Your irreverence toward my deity." —Ambrose Bierce

"When one reality is not permitted to disturb another one, it is one of the first signs of totalitarianism." —Azar Nafisi

"Too much idealism can blind a leader to reality as surely as too much ideology can." —Maureen Dowd

Prejudice: Racial Superiority is a Mere Pigment of the Imagination

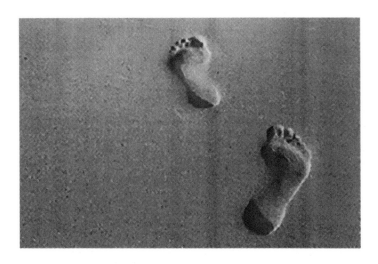

Man or Woman? Black or White? Asian or Latino?
Muslim, Jew, Christian, Buddhist, Hindu, Sikh, or Atheist?

"All looks yellow to a jaundiced eye."
—Alexander Pope

There is no one as blind as the one who does not want to see. —Mexican

"To travel is to discover that everyone is wrong about other countries." —Aldous Huxley

"If you reject the food, ignore the customs, fear the religion, and avoid the people, you might better stay at home." —James A. Michener

There is no discrimination in the forest of the dead.
—Annang, Nigeria

"The darkest thing about Africa has always been our ignorance of it." —George Kimble

Prejudice is the child of ignorance. —Latin

If you open the eyes of a blind man, he wants to go back to darkness. —Berber, North Africa

"To like an individual because he's black is just as insulting as to dislike him because he isn't white." —e.e. cummings

"All colors will agree in the dark." —Francis Bacon

He who knows little judges everything by the one thing he knows. —Japanese

"To live anywhere in the world today and be against equality because of race or color is like living in Alaska and being against snow." —William Faulkner

"We fear things in proportion to our ignorance of them." —Titus Livius

Don't judge a tree by its bark. —French

"Minds are like parachutes: they only function when they are open." —Sir James Dewair

Opinions founded on prejudice are always sustained with the greatest violence. —Hebrew

"The mind of a bigot is like the pupil of the eye: the more light you pour upon it, the more it will contract."
—Oliver Wendell Holmes

***

"Prejudice is being down on something you're not up on."
—Anonymous

Brad, a law student from Indiana, complained to me that Asian students at International House made "disgusting" slurping sounds when they eat noodles or drink soup. His negative cultural associations with the sound prevented him from understanding that slurping has different meanings and associations across cultures. Not only did he avoid sitting with Asian students at meals, he didn't befriend any. His prejudice reminds me of the Turkish proverb: *"If your mouth has been burned with hot milk, you blow before you eat yogurt."*

A negative experience with a few people can lead one to cut off an entire group, as was captured by Mark Twain: *"If a cat sits on a hot stove, that cat won't sit on a hot stove again. That cat won't sit on a cold stove, either; that cat just won't like stoves."*

Brad continued avoiding students from all over Asia, even though many Asians and Americans of Asian descent lived on his floor, and all students shared common shower facilities. A Chinese proverb describes his prejudice: *"Once bitten by a snake, one is forever afraid at the mere sight of a rope."*

During the winter break, most students left. Brad was confined to his room with high fever and a hacking cough.

One morning he heard a knock. He opened his door and two residents, one Japanese and the other Chinese, greeted him, saying they heard he was sick. They handed him a breakfast tray and a large thermos of hot tea.

That moment of kindness was a turning point. Months later, I saw Brad in the dining room, slurping noodles with several friends from Asia.

***

Rabbi Jonathan Sacks, in *The Dignity of Difference*, wrote:
> A primordial instinct going back to humanity's tribal past makes us see difference as a threat. That instinct is massively dysfunctional in an age in which our several destinies are interlinked.

Just as the natural environment depends on biodiversity, so the human environment depends on cultural diversity, because no one civilization encompasses all the spiritual, ethnic and artistic expressions of mankind.

Many, from a variety of times and places, have also expressed these ideas:

> *A lot of different flowers make a bouquet.* —Arabic

> *"Being with people just like you is running in a cul-de-sac; it never gets you anywhere."* —Bill Moyers

> *The broad-minded see the truth in different religions; the narrow-minded see only the differences.* —Chinese

> *"The world is a book, and those who don't travel read only a page."* —Saint Augustine

"Mixed company moderates; like-minded company polarizes. Heterogeneous communities restrain group excesses; homogeneous communities march towards extremes." —Bill Bishop

"We must learn to live together as brothers or perish together as fools." —Martin Luther King, Jr.

"The different, the displaced, the refugees are the ones who enrich all our lives, and your tolerance and openness towards them will open new worlds for you, and make you welcome wherever you go." —Kofi Annan

Beyond Our Shores

If we can see beyond ourselves, we can discover the meaning and value of difference. As Andre Gide put it: *"Man cannot discover new oceans unless he has the courage to lose sight of the shore."*

Returning to the Japanese Zen parable that began our journey together, I remember the frog. Only after leaving the pond could it finally see water. Similarly, only by experiencing other cultures, could I see my own culture in new ways.

Two tadpoles are swimming in a pond. Suddenly, one turns into a frog and jumps out of the pond.

When the frog returns to the pond, the tadpole sees the frog and asks, "Where did you go?"

"I went to a dry place," answers the frog. "What is 'dry'?" asks the tadpole.

"Dry is where there is no water," says the frog.

"And what is 'water'?" asks the tadpole.

"You don't know what 'water' is?" the frog says with disbelief. "It's all around you! Can't you see it?"

When we are not prepared, or too frightened, to leave our small cultural ponds, our "distorted" perceptions of other realities can lead to misunderstandings and faulty conclusions. As Friedrich Nietzsche wrote, *"Those who were seen dancing were thought to be insane by those who could not hear the music."*

Let us open our minds and hearts, discover the music, hear it clearly, and join the dance.

Questions and Activities, Chapter Six

1. Consider the example of the surgeon who could not operate on "...this boy because he's my son!" For men, can you think of any examples where you would find it difficult to imagine a particular job being done by a woman? What types of jobs occur to you; and what do your female friends, colleagues or classmates think of your responses? For women, are there certain types of jobs that you find it difficult to imagine being done by a man? What do your male friends, colleagues or classmates think of your responses? In what respects do you think your responses reflect gender roles as defined by your culture? Interview a man and a woman

born and raised in at least two different countries other than your own. How do their responses about gender roles compare and contrast with yours? Ask if their responses reflect or at odds with the general patterns in their countries.

2. Log on to your *Cultural Detective Online* subscription and click on the *Women and Men* Package. Review the "Introduction to Women and Men" in the Overview. Then interview a man and a woman from a culture different than your own; ask them how their cultures define appropriate ways to be feminine and masculine. How are these definitions different from your own, and how do they compare and contrast with those of classmates, friends or colleagues from other cultures?

3. In your *Cultural Detective Online* subscription, proceed to the *Global Diversity & Inclusion* Package, where you'll find the "Gender and Peace Keeping Operations" incident. After reviewing the incident and filling in the Worksheet, compare your perspectives with those of Sanjay, the Indian husband, and Anuradha, the Indian wife. Be sure to scroll right in the Worksheet, to reflect not only on national cultural differences, but also on gender roles and values around diversity and inclusion. Discuss possible ways of resolving the conflict with your classmates, colleagues or friends, and compare your responses with the Author Ideas in the Cultural Bridges section.

4. Consider the proverbs in Chapter Six that refer to prejudice or discrimination. Describe how one or more of the proverbs illustrate a prejudice or an act of

discrimination you have experienced or witnessed. Discuss with classmates, friends or colleagues their experiences with prejudice and discrimination. What are some of the possible causes of prejudice or discrimination in these cases? Can you think of examples that illustrate the Mexican proverb, "There is no one as blind as the one who does not want to see?" What are some strategies that might help to counter or limit acts of prejudice and discrimination?

CHAPTER SEVEN

Globalization and its Disconnects:
Convergence without Context

The increasing speed of globalization, fueled by technology and explosive migrations across borders, is producing spiraling cultural contacts without context. Individuals with vastly different experiences and assumptions are thrust together without preparation. The result is often heightened misperceptions, miscommunications and polarization across cultures.

***

"Don't trust everything you see. Even salt looks like sugar."
— Maryum Ahsam

Shortly after the ISIS terrorist attack on Barcelona during the summer of 2017, a Spanish university student arrived at UC Berkeley, his first experience in the United States. A week after he had moved into International House, he noticed from his window several bearded men with turbans who were handing out flyers. Alarmed, he told his U.S. American roommate that ISIS was out distributing propaganda on the street. The roommate decided to go outside to check out the content of the flyers while his roommate, still haunted by the attack in Spain, chose to wait anxiously in the room. The U.S. American took one of the flyers, which encouraged people to help feed the homeless. In chatting with one of the bearded men, he realized they were from the Sikh community, whose religion encourages service to the poor and others in need. Not having had any knowledge of or experience with Sikhs, the Spanish student was relieved to learn of the encounter, and he was intrigued when his roommate him about his very first conversation with someone from the Sikh community, who was also a student at UC Berkeley; she told him that while Sikhs pronounce their identity in the United States as "seeks," in their traditional Punjabi language and among themselves, they pronounce Sikh as "sick." When first introducing herself, she said, "I'm 'sick' but not contagious!"

Just as the Spanish student's misperception of the bearded

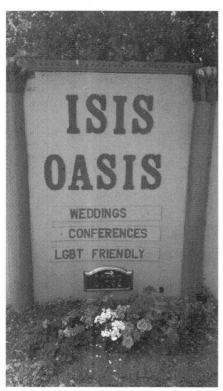

and turbaned men in Berkeley was driven by a single experience, imagine how many travelers in a rural part of Northern California might react when encountering a large, colorful roadside sign which reads, "ISIS OASIS."

Isis Oasis is a place for weddings and conferences, and it's "LGBT friendly!" How could that be? Yet for most people familiar with ISIS as the terrorist "Islamic State of Iraq and Syria," Isis, the ancient Egyptian goddess of life, does not spring to mind.

The blog "Glossophilia," dedicated to discussing the English language in all its usage, recently questioned whether every "Isis" on the planet—referring to ships, rivers, companies, software programs, scientific references or persons, named for the Egyptian goddess of life and womanly strengths—should be expected to rebrand themselves for fear of being stained by the sins of a deadly mission. That is why ISIS—the Institute for Science and International Security—a nuclear non-proliferation think tank, is encouraging the world's media not to use the "ISIS" acronym when referring to the terrorist group, but rather to choose "ISIL"—the Islamic State of Iraq and the Levant.

Just as "ISIS" does not easily communicate its varied meanings and associations, so the forces of globalization often create perception challenges for global companies whose brands do not automatically translate across cultures. According to an article in *Marketing Magazine*, Starbucks' support for the LGBT community puts it at odds with local customs in some societies. The article suggests that "...the brand is placed at the intersection of a cultural struggle between cosmopolitan global discourses and local forces which feel cornered by the messages of globalization; and so Starbucks' stand for gender diversity has met fierce opposition in Indonesia and Malaysia, where religious groups have proposed boycotting Starbucks in retaliation for its support of LGBT rights."[1]

The rapid crossing of products across cultures can present political as well as religious challenges. When, for example, Procter and Gamble's powder detergent was marketed in Germany a few years ago, it was promoted with the number 88 on the label, suggesting that the package was sufficient to handle 88 loads—five more than the traditional eighty-three. Yet many shocked Germans perceived the neo-Nazi code for Hitler as "H," which is the eighth letter of the alphabet. Reactions were similar to the liquid detergent packaging that was promoted with "18," the number of loads the bottle could support. In this case, many outraged and protesting Germans saw the number one, the first letter of the alphabet, as code for Adolph. As a result, Procter and Gamble stopped shipping the offending powder and liquid detergents to Germany.[2]

Because of ISIL terrorist attacks in various non-Muslim and Muslim countries by those who claim to be acting in the name of Islam, fear and stereotyping of *all* Muslims and those who appear to come from the Middle East have increased in frightening ways.

> *"The problem is that perception is reality."*
> —John Rowland

In the midst of the 2016 U.S. presidential election, soon after the idea of a Muslim ban was introduced by Donald Trump, a disturbing incident of misperception took place on an American Airlines flight. A man with dark olive skin, curly hair and a foreign accent was quietly writing on a notepad before the plane took off. A female passenger sat next to him and tried to engage him in conversation, but he deflected her questions and continued writing in what appeared to her to be foreign lettering. His demeanor, appearance, accent and the writing, which she took to be in Arabic, caused her to pass a note to the flight attendant suggesting that he was a likely terrorist. The man was soon taken off the plane and questioned. His credentials revealed that he was an Associate Professor at the University of Pennsylvania and the mysterious notes he was scribbling were equations! Later, it was discovered that he had earned a prestigious medal given to the best Italian economist under 40.[3] Yes, an Italian who, from his appearance, could well have originally been from any number of places in Europe, Latin America, or Iowa or any of the other 49 states!

Donald Trump's relentless attacks on the trade policies of China during the presidential campaign have had a painful impact on U.S. Americans of Asian descent. Michael Luo, a son of immigrant parents from China and a reporter for the *New York Times*, was leaving church on Manhattan's Upper East Side one Sunday when a woman yelled at him, "Go back to China!" The impact was perhaps the more searing as Mr. Luo's seven-year-old boy kept asking, "Why did she say 'Go back to China?' We're not from China."[4]

With globalization, many of the new contacts between people of different ethnic and national backgrounds produce marriages; yet because these inter-ethnic relationships are still unusual for people in many places in the world, it's still common for people to have misconceptions about them. Recently, a Caucasian professor at a South Korean university was being interviewed in his home in Seoul for BBC television. During the interview, a little girl entered the room, followed shortly after by a crying baby crawling toward her sister. Then a panicked Asian-looking woman, the professor's wife, rushed into the room and rapidly took the children from the office. Soon after, a flood of comments on social and major media outlets came to the conclusion that the woman was the professor's nanny.[5]

The incident in Korea reminded me of how the rapid forces of globalization often blind me to what I am unaccustomed to seeing or hearing. Sitting in a cafe in Trieste, Italy during the spring of 2017, I was chatting with a woman of Chinese ancestry who was a dentist practicing in Hungary. She spoke English with an accent that I had heard hundreds of times but was unable to identify. I kept trying to think of where she might be from by the way she was speaking—to no avail. Finally, when I asked her where she was raised, she said India; immediately I recognized a common way of speaking English among many South Asians. But because she told me she was of Chinese ancestry and could certainly have passed for Chinese in appearance, I could not identify the accent. I was locked in a pond that had never experienced a Chinese person speaking in this way.

Approach Life with an Open Mouth

Disruptive contacts between cultures have accelerated with the explosion of migrations across borders; because of abrupt departures from homelands and arrivals in countries with vastly different assumptions about what is normal, misunderstandings abound.

Juan, a Honduran friend, recently spoke to me about a group of twenty Cuban refugees who fled the Castro regime. They arrived by raft with few possessions, exhausted and hungry. After Juan helped them get settled with housing and employment, he asked them if they had any urgent needs. The response was unanimous—they wanted a horse! Stunned, Juan wondered why they needed a horse when transportation in the area was easy. When they reassured him that a horse was not needed for travel, he wondered if they wanted a horse as a pet—perhaps evoking a fond memory of ranches in Cuba. But when they explained that they wanted the horse for food, Juan was stupefied, as horses are not commonly eaten in Honduras. When the Cubans asked for funds to purchase a horse that they would kill and use for a barbecue and other horse recipes, Juan was horrified and refused, but offered to buy them a cow. Little did Juan know that horse meat has traditionally been consumed in Cuba in *Aporreado de Tajajo*, a classic Cuban stew considered a delicacy. Even when the Cubans explained that horse meat is often eaten in France, Belgium and Italy, and is also used for sashimi and to flavor ice cream in Japan, Juan remained unconvinced.

***

> *"People generally see what they look for,*
> *and hear what they listen for."*
> —Harper Lee, *To Kill a Mockingbird*

Entry into a completely unknown culture is generally disorienting, but when refugees fleeing violence, depravation and loss of family arrive in a strange new land the communication challenges can be enormous. According to the *American Family Physician,* the urgent health needs of many refugees are not easily met due to cultural barriers between Western physicians and those from non-Western, hierarchical cultures. In many hierarchical cultures it is uncommon to ask a question of an authority figure such as a physician; and to avoid losing face, patients from these cultures may nod, smile and give the physician the impression that directives are understood even when they are not. The western physician may have no idea that admitting one does not understand may be humiliating for the patient. And while some refugees may expect physicians to cure everything, others may believe that illnesses are an incurable, unavoidable part of life—or that, according to their traditions, they are caused by some unfriendly spirit and can only be cured by shamans with their access to positive spirits.[6] A superb, eye-opening account of such conflicts of perception and the collision of cultures, specifically between Western medical practitioners and the Hmong people originally from Laos, can be found in *The Spirit Catches You and You Fall Down* by Anne Fadiman.

One of the most misunderstood practices among the Hmong and many other communities in Asia is "coin rubbing." It's a way of encouraging body toxins to escape the body by rubbing the skin with a coin, a spoon, or by "cupping," a process by which heat is injected in a cup, then placed on the skin, sometimes producing a bruise when removed. For some Western medical practitioners and many social workers, the appearance of bruises on the body caused by coin rubbing or cupping suggests physical abuse. An oft-repeated story in the Southeast Asian community is one of a well-educated Vietnamese man who was placed in jail for child abuse. This man had practiced coin rubbing to help relieve the fever of his child. The child's fever was not relieved, so the father brought the child to the hospital, where he was accused of child abuse. The man was so embarrassed that people thought he had beaten his child that he killed himself while in jail.[7]

As noted in a recent broadcast on *National Public Radio,* many refugees come from cultures in which people are unaccustomed to having a primary doctor and in which preventative check-ups simply do not exist. Refugee women who come from societies in which Pap smears are either unknown or considered a threat can find the practice particularly sensitive. For those who come from traditional societies in which women are expected to be virgins before they marry, the Pap smear can be perceived as a menace, a test that will break the hymen and thereby make the women ineligible to marry and perhaps cause them to be ostracized from their communities. Western physicians who have treated refugee women from these societies say that it's not infrequent to find undiagnosed cervical cancer in these populations.[8]

Misperceptions about the Pap smear can sometimes be overcome when the gynecologist has cultural links to the refugee community in question and is able to explain the Pap smear's health benefits while showing how the procedure can be administered so as to preserve the hymen.

While it is difficult enough for those born and raised in the United States to understand the U.S. healthcare system, it can be especially problematic for recent refugees and immigrants. Without a shared cultural experience, the possibilities for misinterpretation can be very dangerous—especially in medical emergencies. For example, diagnosing pain can be perplexing for Western emergency responders and medical practitioners. Individuals in some cultures are conditioned to be stoic and remain silent in the presence of severe pain; others may wail when only slightly uncomfortable. According to research at the Baylor University Medical Research Center, many Asian patients rarely ask for pain medication, whereas many patients from areas on the Mediterranean coast seek pain medication for the slightest discomfort. By contrast, in some West African societies, a woman in labor may express her pain with barely an audible sound.[9] Without some sense of the varying ways of expressing pain across cultures, a physician could quite easily miss a complication and ignore a serious underlying problem or perhaps overmedicate someone who expresses pain in alarming, unfamiliar ways.[10]

For those who have experienced torture, many will be particularly sensitive to some types of hospital rooms in their new homelands. Being left alone in small bare rooms, even for short periods of time, may evoke traumatic memories of rooms where they have been tortured, unbeknownst to their Western doctors; in some cases, first time encounters with stethoscopes and blood pressure cuffs have been perceived as instruments of torture.[11]

***

"No two people see the external world in exactly the same way. To every separate person, a thing is what he thinks it is—in other words, not a thing, but a think."
—Penelope Fitzgerald

I remember being surprised during the day and often into the evening in Amsterdam at being able to see into the living rooms and dining areas of many Dutch homes. In some cases, the curtains were left open and in others there were no curtains at all. I could easily see a family enjoying a meal or watching TV. Some Dutch friends told me that this practice could perhaps be explained by Calvinistic roots, that people are demonstrating they have nothing to hide; others dismiss the religious interpretation, saying that in a northern European clime there's simply a hunger for light.

Whatever the explanation, a similar phenomenon can be found in Denmark. Birgitte Demme Larsen, a Danish anthropologist who has studied refugees in rural areas, observed that an African refugee did not realize that closing his curtains during the day was interpreted by locals as being suspiciously secretive. She went on to note that other newcomers did not realize that congregating and talking loudly in a local grocery store was likely to offend Danish sensibilities.[12]

To Talk or Not To Talk

In the German town of Oberhausen, refugees fleeing conflict in Iraq, Syria and Afghanistan, accustomed to greeting each other on buses, are startled by the quiet and lack of conversation among Germans on buses. One refugee from Afghanistan, struggling to understand local customs, wondered whether it was illegal to talk![13]

Many from Middle Eastern capitals are confused when seeing European pedestrians waiting for a green light to cross the street even without a car in sight. They wonder why rules apply to situations that do not appear to require them; and for Muslim asylum seekers, the prevalence of pork and sausage dishes in Denmark, Germany and other European countries is seen as sacrilegious.

Some of the most difficult and dramatic differences in perception in our global and interconnected world involve clashes about the role of women. Many refugees and immigrants come from societies in which the genders are segregated in social settings and where women, and sometimes men as well, cover much of their bodies to express modesty. People from these societies are often shocked when they see European women who are scantily dressed, viewing them as immoral or even as prostitutes. A recent article in *The New York Times* about the German city of Weimar noted that some inebriated refugees lectured female bartenders about the immorality of their work, and then proceeded to follow them home. In response, German student volunteers developed a pamphlet describing German social customs, noting that a greeting hug from a woman did not, as a rule, suggest a sexual invitation.[14] In many European and North American countries there are classes offered to refugees encouraging respect for women and equality of the sexes. Yet, according to an article in *The Economist*,

> "Teaching sexual norms is tricky, though, particularly when European societies do not agree on what those norms should be. In Norway, Ms. Hagen's course uses photos of pop stars to explain that styles of dress, however scanty, are expressions of individual freedom rather than signals of availability and must be respected. At the same time, bizarrely, it coaches male refugees to protect their reputations by not seeking girls who are "easy." Meanwhile, in Wallonia, the French-speaking region of Belgium, an information sheet used in integration classes cites "gallantry" as an ideal: men should open the door for women, carry their heavy bags and offer to help them put on their coats. Plenty of feminists, in Belgium or elsewhere in Europe, would find this patronizing."[15]

The article goes on to explain that while many Europeans may feel anxious that migrants are importing Middle Eastern values, the migrants are also experiencing significant challenges adjusting to European mores. Middle

Eastern migrants in Belgium, both female and male, find local standards for female dress and behavior quite shocking relative to their home countries. In the 2011 cartoon below by New Zealander Malcom Evans, he offers a vivid visual depiction of how dramatically different cultural norms are around female dress. While it goes nearly without saying that male dominance in any culture is no laughing matter, Evans' work underscores how perplexing women themselves might find such starkly varied expectations of what is "appropriate" when "everything covered but her eyes" is contrasted with practically "nothing covered but her eyes."[16]

An Eritrean asylum seeker in Norway noted that he had learned how to read previously baffling signals from women who wear short skirts, smile or simply walk alone at night without an escort. These gains in his cultural literacy were promoted in classes about the values underlying accepted Norwegian behavior, and which usefully dismantled stereotypes by "....avoiding casting migrants in a bad light" and instead presenting "a fictional character called Arne, a native Norwegian, as a model of predatory behavior" while the immigrant main character, Hassan, is "by contrast, introduced as a 'good man' who is 'honest and well liked.'"[17]

Caught Between Two Worlds

In Canada, refugee experiences of dislocation are sometimes made easier with the support of private Canadian sponsors who provide time and dollars to help guide individuals and families through their first year in the country. Though this widespread support facilitates refugee transitions to a new culture, children of refugees generally adapt more quickly to the new culture than their parents; this in turn produces inter-generational tensions. When a Canadian sponsor took a young Syrian girl along with local children to a ballet performance, the Syrian girl came home and begged for ballet lessons, an alarming request for her parents who were unsettled at the prospect of their daughter being seen in revealing dance outfits. Later, when the Canadian sponsors invited their daughter to make gingerbread houses and sing carols, the strictly Muslim parents feared their daughter would be celebrating a Christian holiday.[18] Moreover, the Syrian parents were confused when they discovered that there were Canadian teenagers who stayed out past midnight and moved away from home when they turned eighteen. When their daughter asked to go on a three-day overnight trip with her fifth grade classmates, her father refused, saying he was not an immigrant who was trying to adapt to a new world; he was an immigrant trying to hold on to what had been ripped away from him.[19] While his daughter found much that was fresh and exciting in her new homeland, she was bothered by Canadian divorces and by stories from her classmates about parents who lived in separate homes.[20]

Still, the perception gap between the girl and her parents widened when she sought to participate in Halloween celebrations involving images of skeletons and ghosts. When the daughter was invited to wear a devil's costume, she was curious and felt the experience would be about being frightened in a playful way. The child's mother, however, wondered how her children could celebrate death and horror "...after they had escaped the real thing."[21]

***

To learn more about the traumatic disconnects of another displaced community, I interviewed Khifshi, a Yazidi refugee from northern Iraq who is now living in the United States. She introduced herself to me in this way:

> I am from a community that has its own distinct culture and monotheistic belief. Because our religion has been falsely and tragically misunderstood as devil worship, it has provoked 74 genocide campaigns over the centuries, the most recent in 2014 when ISIS attacked Yazidi areas in northern Iraq. There, ISIS raped Yazidi women, took them as sex slaves, killed our men and brainwashed our children to become terrorists. I fled with family members, eventually arriving in Turkey where we were again threatened by terrorist groups everywhere.

I migrated in September 2016 with some members of my family to the United States through the International Organization for Migration. Other family members are still in Iraq camps suffering greatly, facing terrible hardship, which makes me feel incomplete. I am thinking of them constantly, not knowing if or when I might lose them. It is hard to live somewhere only as a body while your thoughts are somewhere else. So, for me, freedom here does not always feel free.

Khifshi teaches Yazidi children the Kurmanji language, to help them grow into and retain their cultural identity. And to help them and their parents adapt to life in the United States, Khifshi also teaches English as a Second Language.

Yet as young children adapt to the many freedoms of life in the USA, their parents find it increasingly difficult to control them. Exposed to many U.S. American school children who speak in a manner they perceive as rude to their teachers and parents, and who can be exposed to sex, drugs, and alcohol at an early age, the Yazidi youngsters imitate many of these behaviors experienced as shockingly disrespectful by their parents. And to see their children going to school with U.S. American youngsters wearing shorts, tee shirts, and even pajamas is beyond belief for parents who experienced school uniforms and unquestioned respect for teachers and elders in their home country.

Khifshi was particularly struck when a Yazidi father told her about his six-year-old's request for a laptop. When the father explained that the family did not have enough money to get one, the child threw a fit and said she would report her father to her teacher and to the police!

Coming from a culture in which parents have collective responsibility for all their children, Khifshi explained that if a Yazidi parent saw the child of another parent misbehaving, it would be perfectly acceptable to discipline the child for misbehavior or to take care of a child if in distress. So, when Khifshi, one dark lit evening, noticed a three-year-old following her and calling her "Mommy," Khifshi intuitively responded by holding her hand while offering comforting words. From afar, the child's mother saw her child with a strange woman and ran toward them yelling, "What are you doing with my child?" To Khifshi's surprise, the mother abruptly took her child away without a word of thanks.

Khifshi's actions were again misunderstood when she left work on a freezing cold wintry night with a scarf wrapped warmly around her head and over her mouth. When she

got to her car, she was unable to open its frozen doors. She noticed a man sitting in a nearby car and motioned him to help her, but he remained in his car, unmoved by her pleading gestures. Then she remembered that a few days before there had been a gun related robbery in a nearby market. It occurred to her that the man might be afraid to leave his car in this neighborhood, perhaps also because her head and mouth-covering scarf made him think she was a terrorist! So, she took out her car keys, waving them at him in hopes that he would understand her innocent request. Cautiously, he responded, leaving his car, walking slowly toward her with a metal rod that she initially took to be used as a potential weapon. As they spoke, she interpreted his accent to be Mexican which, fueled by anti-immigrant hysteria in the media, made her anxious until he used the rod to pry open the vehicle's door. As the gentleman departed he smiled and called out "Salaam-Alaikum." Khifshi was relieved not to be considered a terrorist, yet disturbed that she was incorrectly identified as Muslim simply because of a scarf on a cold, wintry night.

Other Yazidi women, Khifshi told me, were thought to be Muslim because some of them wore white head scarves. These white scarves are optional, not religious requirements, and symbolize peace in Yazidi culture; they are generally worn by married women. Their black jackets symbolize sadness, injustice and the persecution of the Yazidis. Yet head scarves continue to be widely associated with Muslim women, even though many Muslim women do not wear them, and their significance in other cultures—or in cold weather—varies in ways never imagined.

Through Afghan and American Eyes: Looking at the same thing and seeing something different.

Muhammad Ali Shahidy, who reflects in Chapter Four on his first confusing experience with a sandwich in the United States, holds a bachelor's degree in psychology from Norwich University in Vermont. His field of study is cultural transmission and parenting practices among Afghan immigrants in the U.S., and he plans to pursue a

Ph.D. in psychology. Here, Muhammad continues his exploration of cultural disconnects and discoveries:

> During the initial week of college in Vermont, I met Scott, my first American friend. He seemed very excited to meet an Afghan. Scott thought that because I came from a mountainous country, I might enjoy hiking trails in the area. So, he asked me if I wanted to go hiking with him. With some cautious reservation, I agreed. In Afghanistan, people don't hang out with strangers. Friendships and bonds are mostly formed within a family community or tribe. Most members of the community are raised together and know each other through continuing interactions over the years. So trust is built either through family connections or over extended periods of time. Until a strong bond is built, one can't just go into the woods with a recent acquaintance. While I could not fully trust Scott, I wanted to make new friends and so decided to take a risk.
>
> As we went hiking, the further into the woods we went, I began to panic. I perceived myself to be in the middle of a vast jungle. I was worrying about whether Scott might stab or abduct me, or perhaps sell my organs. You see, kidnapping, human trafficking, and robbery through the use of physical threat are commonplace in remote areas of Afghanistan, where there is little or no security. Growing up in or near such an environment, Afghans develop a mistrust of strangers. That is why I never walked in front of Scott, but always by

his side or behind him, instinctively fearing a possible attack.

Over time, Scott and I have become close friends. We have both learned enormously from our conversations, particularly about cultural differences. Scott became my American cultural guide, introducing me to a myriad of amazing things about U.S. American culture: bonfires, s'mores, country music, beautiful national parks, fishing and kayaking. Similarly, I became a window for him through which he could begin to see an Afghanistan never before imagined—its hospitable people, great history and rich culture.

Jamshid, an Afghan friend, told me that he was astounded when one of his U.S. American classmates asked him how many people he had killed in Afghanistan. Jamshid had never been in battle and grew up in a village east of Kabul where military confrontations were unknown. Even after moving to Kabul with his family, Jamshid was never involved in a military incident. But questions from Jamshid's classmate reflect the media's portrayal of Afghanistan. Most U.S. news agencies focus almost exclusively on conflicts in the country, and it's these reports that shape how most U.S. Americans see Afghanistan. While it's true that my country has gone through several decades of war with continuing military conflicts in specific regions, there are many areas where people live safely and in peace.

Ironically, Jamshid's friend might have been more likely to use or own a gun in the United States, because of its pervasive gun culture. Yet like many Afghans, Jamshid had never touched a gun in his life.

Jamshid was confounded by another cultural misconception when Matt, a different U.S. American friend, offered to bring him tea before beginning a meal in their school's buffet-style dining hall. Delighted, Jamshid quickly accepted the offer and waited until his friend brought him his first cup of American tea. In the Afghan culture, tea is commonly used as a starter drink, and it's always a nice gesture to offer tea to your guests and friends. So Jamshid was excited to see that he was being warmly welcomed by his new friend. When Matt rejoined Jamshid, he gave him a cup of sweetened iced tea. "There is something odd about the tea," thinks Jamshid. He picks up the cup and continues to think, "Why isn't the cup hot? Maybe American cups are so technologically advanced so as to cool cups which hold hot tea." He drinks with caution, and as soon as he finds out that it's *not* hot tea, he's deeply offended.

In our culture, people *never* serve iced tea, or cold tea, or cooled-down tea to others, or even themselves. A cold tea suggests it's an old tea. When Afghans make tea for their guests, they make sure it's fresh, right out of a hot pot. Serving a cold tea in Afghanistan would indicate that the guest is not welcome. Tea is the first welcoming impression a host communicates. The guest can tell whether someone is a good host or not by evaluating the tea's temperature, freshness and aroma." Jamshid did not say anything and continued to sip his iced tea. He was offended because he thought that Matt did not welcome him to the U.S. But as his academic and social life in the U.S. progressed, Jamshid began, little by little, to enjoy sweetened iced tea.

During my junior year in college, I met a new student from Afghanistan. After two years of living in Vermont, as the only Afghan student in my college, I was thrilled to have a new companion. His name is Mohsen. The first thing I did was to introduce him to all my close college friends—one of whom was Justin. After a few weeks of hanging out with me and Mohsen, Justin one day came to me and asked if Mohsen was autistic. Justin got that impression from Mohsen after a series of social events. I was shocked and reassured him that Mohsen was a very healthy, intelligent individual. Justin explained that sometimes Mohsen failed to pick up on some basic social cues. For instance, during one of our friendly gatherings, Justin was on his phone and wanted some personal space, and so withdrew from the group. He sat somewhere at a distance by himself and started texting. But Mohsen jokingly insisted that Justin be part of the group and should put his cell phone away. To Mohsen, the group needs came first. Coming from a very collectivistic society, Mohsen viewed anyone who withdrew from the group as no longer one of its members, as one who had disrespected the collectivity of the gathering. In fact, by insisting Justin return to the group, Mohsen thought he protected Justin from being ostracized by the rest of us. Mohsen's insistence really annoyed Justin who stared coldly at him and then continued to engage with his phone. On similar occasions, Justin would tell a story in which everyone reacted with some emotion, except Mohsen, who failed to pick up on Justin's sarcasm. Justin perceived Mohsen's unresponsive social behavior as autistic. He thought that if Mohsen was not capable of comprehending his social cues, humor, or cultural references, then he must be autistic. But in reality, Mohsen did not understand Justin's references because they were alien to him, which was why he never reacted to them. For instance, obtaining a driver's license in the U.S. is almost a rite of passage. And if a U.S. American college student shares his or her excitement about getting a driver's license with an Afghan, someone like Mohsen might not respond in kind. In Afghanistan, not many families can afford a car, so Afghan students won't understand the significance of this "rite of passage" for their American counterparts. To have asked about these puzzling references would have made Mohsen appear different from Justin and his other American friends; and being different is frowned upon in Afghan collective culture. From Mohsen's perspective, asking questions around "normal" American behaviors would be humiliating, making him look like an ignorant outsider."

What's In a Name?

Recently, when chatting with Ahmad, a Syrian refugee, I told him about a refugee from another country in the Middle East. Her name was Fadwa—a common name in the region—which means "sacrifice for others" in Arabic.

Yet despite an impressive resume, reflecting an extensive background in e-commerce, business development, and the travel industry, plus numerous job applications, she was unable to secure an interview. Her prospective employers associated her name with FATWA and religious fanaticism. Once she changed her name to Fadiwa, interviews came quickly, and she was offered a job within a few weeks.

The story about Fadwa reminded Ahmad about the headline-grabbing news about Jihad Abdo who had been a celebrity Syrian actor, known throughout the Middle East for his many films and hundreds of television episodes. After publically speaking out against the Syrian dictator, Bashar al Assad, Jihad Abdo was forced to flee Syria, eventually seeking asylum in the United States. Yet his efforts to secure employment in the film industry, despite decades of acting successes and fluent English, proved to be far more difficult than he imagined. To survive, he worked as a delivery man for pizza and flowers shops. Sensing that most U.S. Americans associated the name "Jihad" with armed struggle and terrorism, he changed it to Jay,[22] and eventually was discovered by film director Werner Herzog. The successful audition with Herzog in turn led to prominent acting roles with Nicole Kidman and Tom Hanks. Ahmad explained that the name Jihad is not an uncommon name in the Middle East; and while it can certainly have military or even terrorist associations, it is also often associated not with armed battle but with a struggle for self-empowerment, self-control, and overcoming anger, greed, hatred, and pride. A striking irony about the story of Jihad Jay Abdo is that he is a secularist, respecting all faiths and following none.[23] One of the significant facts about the name Jihad is that it can be found among Christians as well as Muslims in the Middle East. According to Jihad Soailick, a Christian journalist, "...it wasn't Muslims who began using 'Jihad' as a name. In fact, it was begun by Lebanese Christians; and funny enough, the term was actually used to describe their struggle for justice under the Muslim Ottoman Empire."[24]

As I was doing research about the name "Jihad," a friend told me of a Jewish man who had lost all urgent, lifesaving medications in a massive fire in Northern California. His doctor was unavailable because his home and records were lost in the fire. When my friend tried to get the Jewish man's prescriptions renewed, he was blocked due to lack of evidence and various health insurance requirements. Finally, an empathetic physician cut corners to save the man's life. His name? ...Dr. Jihad!

Tarek, another Syrian refugee, told me that in Syria it's quite common and perfectly acceptable for someone to pick up, kiss, and tousle the hair of a stranger's child. A cultural misunderstanding about this was illustrated in a recent news article from Scotland in which a local mom became hysterical when a Syrian refugee approached her one-year-old daughter on a beach and joyfully hoisted her up in his arms.[25] I shared the Scottish story with Tarek, who shook his head sadly, saying he had a similar encounter with a U.S. American woman at a local beach in Northern California. In both encounters, the police were called and were finally able to discover the innocent intent behind the Syrians' behavior. Later I asked Muhammed, an immigrant friend from Iraq, if picking up a stranger's children is common in Iraq. He smiled sadly, saying that it is a common practice in his homeland, but now, after more than ten years living the United States, he has become increasingly uncomfortable when recent Iraqi immigrants or refugees pick up and pat the head of his own child.

For a completely different reason, one should avoid touching or patting the head of a Hmong child. In the Hmong community, it is believed that the head is sacred because it houses an individual's soul. Kathy, a UC Berkeley student in social work, comes from Merced, California, where many of the children of Hmong refugees live. She told me of primary school teachers in Merced who had often expressed affection for their students by patting their heads until anxious children and alarmed parents protested the misinformed behavior. Kathy's own research revealed that in one instance the Hmong children's reverence for the head prevented them from completing a coloring assignment in which various parts of the body would be indicated by a different color. All body parts were generally labeled with the appropriate colors except for various parts of the face and head, which were left untouched, completely blank.

Transformations

The first arrival of Somali refugees in the small former mill town of Lewiston, Maine was met with widespread hostility and resentment. Locals perceived the newcomers as welfare freeloaders.[26] Yet over the years, most of the Somali refugees and other asylum seekers from Chad, Djibouti and Congo demonstrated a desire to succeed with hard work and determination; they slowly helped to transform a town that was badly in need of revitalization in the wake of closed textile plants and widespread unemployment. In 2016, according to a recent *Huffington*

Post blog, despite lingering racial and religious bias, there were former refugees who worked in health care and financial services, even the police force; and many shops have reopened under Somali ownership.[27] The town was brought together in powerful ways in 2015 when the high school soccer team, with seven players who had once languished in Somali refugee camps, won the state championship. Two weeks after the victory, at a party to mark the occasion, a local Somali leader reflected on the crowd that had come to celebrate: "It was so diverse. This is who we are. The whites, the blacks, the young, the old, women, children, men—all of us were there to celebrate our boys!"[28]

***

"Since we cannot see reality,
let us change the eyes which see reality."
—Nikos Kazintzakis

Because increasing contact with refugees and other immigrants fuels fear, misunderstanding, and xenophobia among many born and raised in the United States, it is important to hear and share positive stories like those of Lewiston, Maine. Its story only begins to hint at other largely buried but inspiring contributions of newcomers to the United States. Consider these stunning statistics cited by Bret Stephens, a conservative columnist for *The New York Times*:

- "Non-immigrants start business at half the rate of immigrants and accounted for fewer than half the companies started in Silicon Valley between 1995 and 2005."

- "Just 17 percent of the finalists in the 2016 Intel Science Talent Search—often called the 'Junior Nobel Prize'—were the children of United States-born parents. At the Rochester Institute of Technology, just 9.5 percent of graduate students in electrical engineering were non-immigrants."[29]

Another *New York Times* columnist, Frank Bruni, cites additional immigrant achievements that are generally unrecognized.

- "The United States has had more than 350 Nobel Prize winners. More than 100 of these have been immigrants and individuals born outside the United States."
- Cecilia Conrad, head of the MacArthur Foundation Genius Grant program, noted that immigrants were overrepresented among "winners of the Pulitzer Prize for music, the National Humanities Medal, and especially of the Jolen Bates Clark medal, which recognizes brilliant economists under the age of 40. Thirty-five percent of these economists were foreign born."
- Of the 935 MacArthur Fellows Genius awards, "209 were born outside the United States."

Frank Bruni reveals that some of the MacArthur grantees have been refugees. None of this is surprising to him and Cecilia Conrad, who credit the different perspectives and life experiences of newcomers as promoting fresh ideas, inventions, "...and discoveries nourished by the experience of dislocation and navigating a new culture and a new set of norms."[30]

Other striking misperceptions of immigrants are revealed by a Cato Institute study, noting that non-immigrants are incarcerated at almost twice the rate of illegal immigrants and at more than three times the rate of legal ones; and the rate of criminality among non-immigrant teens far exceeds that of their immigrant peers.[31]

***

"Most misunderstandings in the world could be avoided
if people would simply take the time to ask,
'what else could this mean?'"
—Shannon L. Adler

As globalization thrusts cultures, languages and symbols together as never before, technology responds with computerized translations designed to facilitate communication among people who speak different languages. Yet because the very same word may have a different meaning or connotation across languages, and as styles of speaking, tone and inferences often cannot be accurately translated by a person, let alone by a computer, errors can be made that have unintended, startling and disturbing consequences. For example, in 2015 a local Spanish town threatened to sue Google when its computerized translation translated a word in the Galician language of northern Spain for a leafy green vegetable as "clitoris."[32] As a result, the town's annual green vegetable festival was promoted as the "clitoris" festival—something the local townspeople didn't believe when announced![33]

Just the other day, a successful business executive and former refugee from El Salvador told me he could not understand why many business colleagues in several Latin and Mediterranean countries were not able to respond to his requests for information "ASAP," which he assumed would translate across languages while communicating virtually. The business executive, now in the United States for 15 years, had become accustomed to what "ASAP" suggests for many in the United States—a sense of urgent need, perhaps today, but not later than a day or two. So when the "ASAP" requests seemed to be ignored for several days, weeks, or occasionally even months, he was frustrated, angry and at a loss for an explanation. Finally, he remembered that many in El Salvador took it to mean literally "as soon as possible."

That is, it will be done when it is possible, perhaps after an extended time with family, after a variety of other more important projects are completed, or whenever it suits the person in question.

One can appreciate the serious diplomatic implications of inadequate computer translations when considering these recent, since corrected, Google translations:

- "Russian Federation" translated as "Lord of the Rings"
- "Russians" translated as "Occupiers"
- "Sergey Lavrov"—the Russian foreign minister—translated as "sad little horse"[34]

It's the absence of the ability to interpret context, nuance, tone, irony or sarcasm that makes computer translations especially problematic. How, for example, would a computer accurately convey the meaning of "head," which as a noun could signify a leader, a slang term for toilet, the body part above the neck, white bubbles in beer, or a place where a river begins, any of which could be confused with the verb meaning to go in a particular direction, or to be in control of a group, to be first in line or to hit a ball with one's head?

Recognizing the ongoing challenges for human translation professionals helps us to become especially sensitive to the inevitable perils of machine translations. For instance, it was reported that Donald Trump told a European Commission meeting that "the Germans are bad, very bad." The German media did not know what to make of this, debating whether Trump meant that the Germans were "böse"—evil—or "schlecht," meaning they were not doing the right thing.[35]

So, while technology attempts to cope with translation challenges in an increasingly globalized economy, there is as well a heightened need for human beings with bilingual skills. According to the Foundation for Young Australians, for example, advertisements for jobs requiring bilingual skills grew by 181% from 2012 to 2015.[36] And according to a 2016 U.S. Bureau of Labor Statistics report, there will be a 17% increase in translation job opportunities by 2026, much faster than the average for all occupations.

"TMI," a common text expression meaning "too much information," and "FOMO," signifying a "fear of missing out," are symptoms of today's need to address and manage the explosion of information released by technology. Devices that attempt to instantaneously translate languages are complemented by the rapid development of emojis and emoticons designed to convey emotion and meaning in visual shorthand. In the same way that verbal and written languages do not easily translate across cultures, so images and symbols involve similar problems. A bowing icon, for example, is generally appreciated and felt differently in Asian countries than in Western societies; while visual images representing hugs and kisses can be interpreted variously in different cultural communities. Imagine the implications for discussions across cultures about sexual harassment! A specific emoji for illness was interpreted by French Canadians as "bicep implants," whereas the same image was perceived by Arabic experts as "smelly armpits."[37] And the emoji for "face with tears of joy" was interpreted positively by some and negatively by others.[38]

Emoticons or symbols for emotion are generally expressed vertically in East Asian countries and read top to bottom. Because emotional control is generally an important value in East Asia, face-to-face emotions and digital emoticons subtly convey emotional cues in the eyes, not readily understood by many Westerners. By contrast, Western emoticons are read horizontally, emphasizing open emotional expression in the mouth.[39] That is perhaps why so many Asians often find U.S. American smiles, in particular, to be so bewildering. If the meaning of a smile is difficult to translate across cultures, consider how a smile is portrayed among different devices and operating systems:

These are all the same emoji!

This is what the "grinning face with smiling eyes" emoji looks like on devices for each of these platforms:

Apple   Google   Microsoft   Samsung   LG   HTC   Twitter   Facebook   Mozilla   Emoji One

"This emoji, the researchers found, is among the most commonly misinterpreted, with a significant variation in interpreted meaning from different device users."[40]

Is it any wonder then that a global firm called "Today Translations" early in 2017 was looking to hire an emoji translator?![41]

***

Awareness of the need for enhanced understanding across languages and cultures has been growing for many decades. Almost forty years ago, in response to a 1979 U.S. Presidential Commission on Foreign Languages and International Studies, I conducted a study on the shocking ignorance and incompetence of U.S. Americans in their interactions with other countries. Some of these published findings in 1981 and 1982 shed light on why, since then, we have had so many misperceptions about the world around us; the legacy and facts of many of these 1981-82 findings remain to this day.[42, 43]

Almost forty years after my initial findings, it is disappointing that global literacy has not significantly improved. Meanwhile, the forces and speed of globalization create a far more urgent need for understanding across cultures.

Given today's growing fear of immigrants and refugees in the United States, it's noteworthy that only 34% of U.S. university students realize that more Mexicans have left the United States than entered it in the last five years; and only 57% were able to identify Sudan as being located in Africa![44] In 2016, the Council on Foreign Relations and *National Geographic* commissioned a survey to assess the global literacy of U.S. American college students; only 30% of the over 1200 students who participated earned a passing grade. The remaining 70% were found by U.S. American education leaders to be globally incompetent, lacking the capacity and disposition to understand and act on issues of global significance.[45]

Based on a recent analysis of the U.S. Government Accounting Office, 23% of language-designated overseas positions for the Department of State were filled by Foreign Service Officers who did *not* meet the positions' language proficiency requirements, and there were especially *severe* shortages for languages spoken in China, Iran, India, Korea and various countries in the Middle East. Such shortages have affected the ability to communicate effectively with foreign and diplomatic audiences. For example, a Foreign Service Officer reported that when the embassy in Cairo hosted a Ramadan cultural event, Foreign Service Officers were generally not able to communicate in Arabic with Egyptian attendees, including government officials and local media contacts.[46]

The continuing foreign language deficit in the United States is unsurprising when one considers that only 7% of U.S. college students are enrolled in a language course; and of those who are enrolled in foreign language courses, the vast majority were in European languages.[47] Unlike many other parts of the world, the United States does not require its K-12 students to learn a second language, and as recently as 2010 only about half of higher education institutions required foreign language study for a baccalaureate—this in a world where only a quarter of the world's population speaks English.[48]

Overall ignorance and misunderstanding of other countries and cultures in the United States is reflected in the fact that only 36% of U.S. Americans own passports as opposed to 60% in Canada, 80% in the U.K., and 50% in Australia.[49] Because only 10% of U.S. states require high school students to take a geography course for graduation, it's no wonder that U.S. Americans of all ages have consistently scored lower than citizens of other countries on knowledge of geography and current events.[50] While universities do offer classes in geography and international studies, such courses are, as a rule, not required, if not part of a major field of study.[51]

***

"I find that because of modern technological evolution and our global economy, and as a result of the great increase in population, our world has greatly changed: it has become much smaller. However, our perceptions have not evolved at the same pace; we continue to cling to old national demarcations and the old feelings of 'us' and 'them'."
—Dalai Lama

To meet the challenges of growing global interdependence in the early 1980s, international educators lobbied for dramatic increases in required international and foreign language courses. But today, while there continues to be a pressing need for a massive increase in these courses, traditional approaches to international education are insufficient to address the growing intercultural disconnects produced by unprecedented migrations, globalization and the explosion of information. The sheer speed with which the information is communicated, by necessity in abbreviated ways, often results in misunderstanding, fear and polarization.

In order to cope with globalization and its disconnects, there is a compelling need for developing intercultural competence in schools and in virtually every profession that involves working across cultures. Aside from offering culture specific information, intercultural competence courses and training sessions enable individuals to become aware of their own values and biases, which drive specific behaviors and shape perceptions and misperceptions of those who are culturally different. At the same time, individuals are trained to view their own values and behaviors through the eyes of those from varying cultural backgrounds. In the process, we can learn to identify and understand varying communication styles, approaches to politesse and power, time and touch, gesture and gender, religion and righteousness, right and wrong, etc., etc., etc. In essence, intercultural competence encourages us to pause, suspend judgment, and ask, "What *else* could that startling behavior mean?" With globalization's bewildering flood of new contacts and information, I often reflect that the closer we get to each other, the further apart we often become. But indispensable bridges across these troubled waters can be built with cross-cultural skills that help to transcend the fear of difference, while fostering communication and understanding across cultural divides.

"The two words 'information' and 'communication' are often used interchangeably, but they signify quite different things. Information is giving out; communication is getting through."
—Sydney J. Harris

Questions and Activities for Chapter Seven

1. Interview a refugee and/or someone who works for a refugee support group in your community. From their experiences, what are some specific examples of cultural disconnects or misunderstandings between refugees and those who are working to support them in your community? What are some of the particular differences in lifestyle, values and behaviors between the refugees' home countries and yours that help to explain the cited cultural disconnects? What have been some successful strategies for bridging differences between refugees and members of their host community?

   (To help raise awareness of the powerful challenges faced in the migrant experience, a skilled facilitator might be engaged to conduct the downloadable game, "On The Road With Migrants," produced by Caritas France and available in French, English, German, Greek, Italian, and Spanish with a link at: https://blog.culturaldetective.com/2015/06/16/on-the-road-with-migrants-game/.)

2. To explore cultural identity issues, log on to your *Cultural Detective Online* subscription, and review the Overview introduction for the *Cultural Detective Blended Culture* package. Then consider the 23-minute movie, "Migrants Moving History: Narratives Of Diversity In Europe" at: www.migrants-moving-history.org.

   Share your reactions to the film and questions about cultural identity with classmates, friends and colleagues who were born, raised and/or who have experienced extended periods of time in other countries. What are some of the challenges and benefits for individuals who are influenced by multiple cultural experiences?

3. What are your preferred social media platforms and why have you chosen them? In what respects have they facilitated and/or created miscommunications for you across cultures and within your own culture? Compare how you use social media with individuals from at least three different regions of the world. What are some of the similarities and differences you have discovered? What are some specific examples of the benefits as well as the dangers of instantaneous communication using social media in a globalizing world?

4. Review the story in Chapter Seven about the Syrian refugee family in Canada and the tension between their traditional way of life and the western influences on their young daughter. Interview someone raised in your country whose parents came as refugees. What are some of the cultural conflicts created between the parents and your interviewee? How has the interviewee managed to navigate these conflicts?

5. Explore generational differences within the same country and culture by logging on to the *Cultural Detective Generational Harmony* Package in *Cultural Detective Online*. After reviewing the values and characteristics of five generations in the United States in the "Overview" section, consider "Media Influences on Five Generations" in the "Supplementary Material" section. Then, review the Values Lenses for each of the five generations. See if the lenses and the media influences for your generation and that of your parents, and/or your children, offer

explanations about generational differences and perhaps disconnects that you may have experienced. What techniques have you used, or might you consider using to bridge the generational differences?

If you were born and raised in a country other than the United States, in what specific ways has globalization and technology in your country created differences between generations? In what respects are the generational differences described for the United States similar and/or different from those in your country?

Notes

1. Dr. Bernardo Fiqueiredo and Natalia Perara, "Brands at the intersection of global and local cultures," *Marketing Magazine*, August 11, 2017.

2. "Detergent pulled in Germany over Neo-Nazi code," Associated Press, May 9, 2014.

3. Catherine Rampell, "Ivy League economist ethnically profiled, interrogated for doing math on American Airlines flight," *Washington Post*, May 7, 2016.

4. Michael Luo, "An open letter to the woman who told us: 'go back to China,'" *The New York Times*, October 11, 2016.

5. Caroline Davis, "BBC interview hijacked by children prompts social media debate," March 12, 2017.

6. D. S. Kay, "Cultural aspects of caring for refugees," *American Family Physician*, March 15, 1998.

7. Mary Jo Beghtol, "Hmong refugees and the U.S. health system," *Cultural Survival Magazine*, March 1988.

8. Sarah Varney, "For some refugee women, health care is a culture shock," *Kaiser Health News,* September 28, 2017.

9. Mary Moore Free, "Cross-cultural conceptions of pain and pain control," *Baylor University Medical Proceedings*, April 15, 2002.

10. Clifford Fram, "Doctors at risk of misunderstanding pain," *The Australian*, May 3, 2013.

11. Heidi Shin, "Massachusetts clinic treats refugees with mindfulness and medicine from home," *Yes! Magazine*, March 20, 2016.

12. David Zucchino, "'I've become a racist': migrant wave unleashes Danish tensions over identity," *The New York Times*, September 5, 2016.

13. Howard Johnson and Tobias Brauer, "Migrant crisis: changing attitudes of German city," BBC News, April 28, 2016.

14. Rick Lyman and Marissa Eddy, "Welcome to Weimar," *The New York Times*, May 24, 2017.

15. "Europe is trying to teach its gender norms to refugees," *The Economist*, October 15, 2016.

16. *Ibid.*

17. Andrew Higgens, "Norway offers immigrants a gentle lesson on how to treat women," *The New York Times*, December 15, 2015.

18. Catrin Einhorn and Jodi Kantor, "A Syrian child transformed," *The New York Times*, December 18, 2016.

19. *Ibid.*

20. *Ibid.*

21. *Ibid.*

22. Andrew Anthony, "Jay Abdo, Syrian actor: how I changed my name from Jihad to Jay and (eventually) conquered Hollywood," *The Guardian*, June 15, 2014.

23. *Ibid.*

24. Jihad Soaileck, "My name is Jihad too!" *Amman News*, April 9, 2010.

25. Sarah Hilley, "Troon Beach social media row after mum shares fury over Syrian refugee 'lifting up' her daughter on shore," *Daily Record*, August 11, 2017.

26. Don Dahlen, "After a bumpy start, Maine town embraces African immigrants," CBS News, April 25, 2016.

27. Cynthia Anderson, "Isbedal: a Maine mill town and the 5000 refugees who call it home," *Huffington Post* Politics blog, December 12, 2015.

28. *Ibid.*

29. Bret Stephens, "Only mass deportation can save us," *The New York Times*, June 17, 2017.

30. Frank Bruni, "Want geniuses? Welcome immigrants," *The New York Times*, September 24, 2017.

31. Bret Stephens, "Only mass deportation can save us," *The New York Times*, June 17, 2017.

32. Ashifa Kassam, "Google translate error sees Spanish town advertise clitoris festival," *The Guardian*, November 3, 2015.

33. *Ibid.*

34. Michael Haugh, "Translation technology is useful, but should not replace learning languages," *The Conversation*, October 15, 2017.

35. Simon Davies, "Can technology replace human interpreters?" *Digitalist Magazine*, January 26, 2017.

36. *Ibid.*

37. Sarah Griffiths, "Can YOU decipher these emoji messages?" Dailymail.com, August 14, 2015.

38. Eyder Peralta, "Lost in translation: study finds interpretation of emojis can vary widely," National Public Radio, April 12, 2016.

39. Sarina Rubinoff, "Face-off: cultural perceptions of emoticons," January 31, 2017.

40. Andrew Hutchison, "Does that emoji mean what you think it means?" *Social Media Today*, April 10, 2016.

41. "You'll need to ace this quiz to become a professional emoji translator," *Vice News*, February 17, 2017.

42. Joseph Lurie, "America Globally Blind, Deaf and Dumb," *Foreign Language Annals*, November 6, 1982.

43. Joseph Lurie, "Xenophobia," *Harper's Magazine – The Public Record*, May 1981.

44. Anna Gawel, "Survey finds U.S. college students' global literacy woefully lacking," *The Washington Diplomat*, December 22, 2016.

45. David Bornstein, "Preparing young Americans for a complex world," *The New York Times*, February 8, 2017.

46. U.S. Government Accounting Office, "Foreign language proficiency has improved, but efforts to reduce gaps need evaluation," March 2017.

47. Amelia Friedman, "America's lacking language skills," *The Atlantic*, May 10, 2015.

48. Zach Simon, "What a Coca-Cola ad taught us about language policy in the U.S.," *Huffington Post*, February 6, 2014.

49. Sanford J. Unger, "American ignorance," *Inside Higher Education*, March 23, 2015.

50. Abigail Montgomery, "Don't know much about geography: Why Americans need a crash course on the forgotten subject," *The Lance*, December 4, 2015.

51. Anna Gawel, "Survey finds U.S. college students' global literacy woefully lacking," *The Washington Diplomat*, December 22, 2016.

AFTERWORD

Bridging Cultures

by Dianne Hofner Saphiere

Seeing can be deceiving, as Joe has shown us. Some cultural differences we've read about seem fairly easy to bridge. Other differences, however, can be subtler or more deceptive.

Serving vegetarian food at a banquet, providing meat options that do not include pork or shellfish, or reserving a room for prayer in an office building do not seem to be so difficult. But what about more complex situations? In Chapter One, Joe told us about Africans who address their elders as "Mama" and "Papa." One time, I was asked to intervene, as a consultant, in a case in which an employee had been fired for lying. Why? He had requested time off for his father's funeral—for the third time!

Cross-cultural competence means we should reflect on our assumptions (in this case, that a person has one father), and demonstrate the curiosity to learn a truth that may differ from ours ("I am sorry to hear that. You took time off last month for your father's funeral. Do you have multiple fathers?"). In this way, we can avoid being "deceived" into firing capable, honest workers simply because their cultural practices are different from our own.

At *Cultural Detective* we say, "There is no such thing as common sense, only cultural sense." Common sense is only "common" to those who share it. Sitting on a toilet vs. squatting over it, addressing one man or multiple men in your life as father— both are common sense, or cultural sense, in different contexts. In Mexico, where we live, my son is blessed with many "uncles," none of whom is related to him by blood. The African proverb, "It takes a village to raise a child," certainly resonates with me.

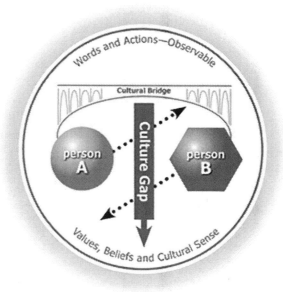

The *Cultural Detective®* Model

In my thirty-five years as a cross-cultural consultant, the most frequent "deception" I encounter is that people try to minimize differences. They ask me to help them "get around" or "get beyond" the differences. However, both my experience and the research on intercultural effectiveness show that when multicultural differences are treated as resources and assets, innovation and creativity are often the result. Inclusive environments and communities with multiple lifestyles help us attract and retain bright, curious people who enjoy and learn from one another.

As with any ability, cross-cultural competence requires practice. Just as we don't become physically fit with one trip to the gym, we need an ongoing, structured way to develop our cross-cultural competence. *Cultural Detective Online* (www.CulturalDetective.com) can provide that approach. We offer frequent complimentary webinars (www.CulturalDetective.Eventbrite.com); please join us and then use a three-day pass to explore the *Cultural Detective Online* system yourself. We also invite you to stay in touch with us via our blog, Twitter, Facebook, and LinkedIn.

Thank you for joining Joe, me, and the *Cultural Detective* Team on this journey of cross-cultural respect and understanding. We firmly believe that together, each of us makes a difference.

***

> *"Never doubt that a small group of thoughtful,*
> *committed citizens can change the world;*
> *indeed, it's the only thing that ever has."*
> —Margaret Mead

INDEX OF STORIES AND PROVERBS BY CULTURE OR GEOGRAPHY

ABOUT THE AUTHOR

Joe Lurie

Joe Lurie is a cross-cultural communication trainer, teacher, and speaker, and Executive Director Emeritus of the University of California, Berkeley's International House, where he served for two decades until 2007. Since then, he's been teaching intercultural communication classes at UC Berkeley and other institutions.

Joe has provided cross-cultural communication training for a variety of clients, including Google, Google.org, Chevron, American Express, the Peace Corps, The Institute of International Education, Tech Women, the World Affairs Council of Northern California, Upwardly Global, Street Smart Brazil, University of Colorado, Tsinghua University in Beijing, and UC Berkeley, among others.

A former Peace Corps Volunteer, he has directed programs in France, Kenya, and Ghana for the School for International Training, and served as Vice President for AFS Intercultural Programs in the USA. He co-authored *Close Encounters of a Cross-Cultural Kind*, and his writings have appeared in *Harper's Magazine*, *U.S. News & World Report*, and *The Mercury News*, and highlighted on National Public Radio. Joe was featured in a national PBS documentary that aired in the U.S. and China and has been interviewed for the Travel Channel.

Joe holds an advanced degree and diploma in African Studies from the University of Wisconsin, Madison, and an M.A. in English from McGill University in Montreal.

Visit the book's website at www.perceptionanddeception.com.

PRAISE FOR *PERCEPTION AND DECEPTION*

"Perception and Deception *offers rich, detailed example after example to demonstrate not only differences across cultures, but the misperceptions that result when we don't have the cultural frame of reference to understand the differences. Further, Lurie makes an excellent case that experiences alone will not automatically lead to understanding and skill development—rather this deeper learning occurs from checking assumptions with others, learning directly from others' experiences, and careful reflection. The guided activities and reflection questions at the end of each chapter are excellent catalysts for this deeper learning. The final chapter, new in this edition, also sheds important light on the complexities of interwoven identities and the urgency of being open-minded in today's world where we interact across multiple cultures without context to guide us. Lurie appropriately concludes the book with a call for the 'compelling need for developing intercultural competence in schools and in virtually every profession that involves working across cultures.'"*
—Barbara Kappler Mikk, Assistant Dean, International Student & Scholar Services, Global Programs and Strategy Alliance, University of Minnesota

***

"This spell-binding book addresses one of the major challenges of the 21st century—making sense, accurately, of global encounters. Lurie's expertise, fascinating stories and wisdom make this a must-read for anyone who crosses cultural borders."
—Joyce Osland, Ph.D., Lucas Endowed Professor of Global Leadership, Executive Director, Global Leadership Advancement Center, School of Global Innovation & Leadership, Lucas College and Graduate School of Business, San Jose State University

Praise for the First Edition

"Don't leave home without it! No, not your credit card, I mean Joe Lurie's master class of miscommunication, Perception and Deception. This is a priceless book for anyone who travels and wants to navigate the minefields of misunderstandings that arise because of cultural differences. A lifetime of practical experience, a compendium of cultural challenges, and a wicked wit combine to make this an indispensable volume for all those planning to step beyond their cultural village. Oh, how I wish this book had been available when I began my international career—how many fewer people I would have inadvertently offended."
—David Lennon, International Vice President of the Association of European Journalists, and a former Managing Editor and Foreign Correspondent for the Financial Times

***

"Joe Lurie is a gifted story teller who has given us a fast, fun-filled read that will transform the way you look at the world and yourself. Perception and Deception reveals much about what's really behind many cultural clashes in work places, schools, and as portrayed in the media."
—Elyse Weiner, Emmy award-winning television network news producer (NBC's Nightly News, ABC's World News Tonight and CNBC)

***

*"*Perception and Deception *is an invitation to be at the table with one of the wisest, most broadly experienced, international interculturalists, whose sense of humor and sense of perspective is revealed in his favorite tales and*

aphorisms from across the globe. It is a truly wonder-filled book. Joe Lurie shares a delicious feast that will long nourish our spirit and soul. Already I can hear the reader calling out to a friend across the room, 'Wait! You've got to hear this!'"
—Dr. John (Jack) Condon, Professor Emeritus, University of New Mexico, and Director, The Jemez Institute

***

"If you are searching for the perfect anecdote to illustrate a point, Joe Lurie has come to the rescue with this engaging collection of intercultural encounters. For the teacher, trainer, speaker, and writer, this is a charming assortment of stories from a wide range of cultures. Examples move through language use and abuse, nonverbal communication, interaction styles, and intercultural conflicts. The tales are accompanied by a rich collection of proverbs from around the world. The reader is alternately amused and shocked, but never bored."
—Dr. Janet Bennett, Executive Director, Intercultural Communication Institute

***

"No matter your background or age, Perception and Deception *will expand your understanding of other cultures (and your own) in astonishing ways. If only I'd had Joe Lurie's intercultural awareness while serving in the diplomatic corps in Asia, Africa, and in Europe, I'd have understood the deeper cultural messages that escape people who hear largely what they're used to hearing and see mostly what they're used to seeing."*
—Ambassador Martin Brennan, Retired

Made in the USA
San Bernardino, CA
19 September 2018